Electronic vs. Floor Based Trading

Zicklin School of Business Financial Markets Conference Series Baruch College, CUNY

Robert A. Schwartz, Editor
Baruch College/CUNY
Zicklin School of Business
New York, NY, USA

Other books in the series:

Schwartz, Robert A., Byrne, John A., Colaninno, Antoinette:
A Trading Desk View of Market Quality
Schwartz, Robert A., Byrne, John A., Colaninno, Antoinette:
Call Auction Trading: New Answers to Old Questions
Schwartz, Robert A., Byrne, John A., Colaninno, Antoinette:
Regulation of U.S. Equity Markets
Schwartz, Robert A., Byrne, John A., Colaninno, Antoinette:
Coping With Institutional Order Flow

Electronic vs. Floor Based Trading

edited by

Robert A. Schwartz
Zicklin School of Business, Baruch College, CUNY

John Aidan Byrne
Traders Magazine

Antoinette Colaninno
Zicklin School of Business, Baruch College, CUNY

 Springer

Library of Congress Control Number: 2005935084

ISBN:10: 0-387-29909-2   e-ISBN-10: 0-387-29910-6
ISBN-13: 978-0387-29909-9   e-ISBN-13: 978-0387-29910-5

Printed on acid-free paper.

Printed in the United States of America.

9 8 7 6 5 4 3 2 1

springeronline.com

Contents

List of Participants

Brooke Allen*	President	MANE Fund Management, Inc.

* At the time of the conference, Mr. Allen was Head, Statistical Arbitrage at Maple Securities.

Matthew Andresen*

* At the time of the conference, Mr. Andresen was on the Board of Directors of Lava Trading.

James Angel	Associate Professor of Finance	Georgetown University
Theodore Aronson	Founder	Aronson+Johnson+Ortiz
Eric Barret	Director, Global Electronic Trading	CIBC World Markets Corp.
George Bodine	Director of Trading	General Motors Investment Management
Michael Buek	Principal	The Vanguard Group
Matthew Celebuski	Managing Director	JP Morgan Securities Inc.
Christopher Concannon	Executive Vice President, Transaction Services	The NASDAQ Stock Market
Paul Davis	Managing Director	TIAA-CREF Investment Management
Thomas Doyle	Institutional Sales	Nutmeg Securities
David Dusenbury	Managing Director	Dionis Capital

Alfred Eskandar	Director of Corporate Strategy	Liquidnet, Inc.
Robert Fagenson	President	Fagenson & Company
Reto Francioni	President and Chairman	SWX Swiss Exchange
William Freund*	Emeritus Professor of Economics	Pace University

*At the time of the conference, Professor Freund was Director of the William C. Freund Center for the Study of Securities Markets.

Adena Friedman	Executive Vice President of Corporate Strategy and Data Products	The NASDAQ Stock Market
Robert Gasser	CEO, NYFIX Millennium	NYFIX Millennium
Allan Grody	President and COO	Financial Intergroup
Puneet Handa	Associate Professor	University of Iowa
William Harts		Banc of America Securities
Christopher Heckman	Managing Director	Investment Technology Group, Inc.
Arthur Hogan	Chief Market Analyst	Jefferies & Company
Catherine Kinney	President & Co-Chief Operating Officer	New York Stock Exchange
Richard Korhammer	CEO and co-Founder	Lava Trading Inc.
Michael LaBranche	Chairman, Chief Executive Officer and President	LaBranche & Co., Inc.
Robert McCooey	President & Chief Executive Officer	The Griswold Company, Inc.
Mary McDermott-Holland	Senior Vice President	Franklin Portfolio Associates
Nina Mehta	Reporter	Traders Magazine
Doreen Mogavero	President & Chief Executive Officer	Mogavero, Lee & Company

| Edward Nicoll | Chief Executive Officer | Instinet Group Inc. |
| William O'Brien* | Senior Vice President, Market Data Distribution | The NASDAQ Stock Market, Inc. |

* At the time of the conference, Mr. O'Brien was COO at Brut, LLC.

| Michael Pagano | Assistant Professor | Villanova University |
| Brett Redfearn* | Senior Managing Director | Bear, Stearns & Co., Inc. |

* At the time of the conference, Brett Redfearn was Senior Vice President at the American Stock Exchange.

| Richard Rosenblatt | Founder, President and CEO | Rosenblatt Securities |
| James Ross* | CEO | MatchPoint Trading Inc. |

*At the time of the conference, Mr. Ross was Managing Director at Burlington Capital Markets.

Craig Rothfeld	COO	W.J. Bonfanti, Inc.
Lanny Schwartz	Executive Vice President & General Counsel	Philadelphia Stock Exchange
Robert Schwartz	Marvin M. Speiser Professor of Finance	Zicklin School of Business, Baruch College
Jamie Selway	Managing Director	White Cap Trading
Robert Shapiro	Director of Trading	Iridian Asset Management
Michael Simon	Senior Vice President & General Counsel	International Securities Exchange
Benn Steil	Director of International Economics	Council on Foreign Relations
Wayne Wagner	Co-Founder & Chairman	Plexus Group
Avner Wolf	Chairman, Economics & Finance Department and	Zicklin School of Business, Baruch College

| Robert Wood | Director, International Programs Distinguished Professor of Finance | University of Memphis |

Conference Sponsors

American Stock Exchange
Archipelago Exchange
Bernard L. Madoff Investment Securities
Instinet Group Inc.
International Securities Exchange
Liquidnet, Inc.
NASDAQ Stock Market
New York Stock Exchange
NYFIX Millennium
Philadelphia Stock Exchange
Plexus Group
Security Traders Association
SWX Swiss Exchange

Preface

This book is a comprehensive account of Electronic vs. Floor Based Trading, the conference hosted by the Zicklin School of Business at Baruch College on May 4, 2004. The text contains the edited transcripts of the panel discussions as well as the keynote speeches by two major industry executives, Edward Nicoll, CEO, Instinet Group, Inc., and Catherine Kinney, President & Co-Chief Operating Officer, New York Stock Exchange

Yet the book is more than an historical record. For one thing, the manuscript has been heavily edited for clarity and unity of ideas. In the process, we introduced new material obtained in interviews after the conference with many of the speakers. Our intention has been to flesh out the discussions while keeping the material as contemporary as possible. In doing so, we were careful not to sacrifice the essential nature of the original debate. For another thing, we have included a paper by Handa, Schwartz, and Tiwari, which is the basis of Puneet Handa's presentation about the relative execution costs of electronically delivered orders and floor broker delivered orders at the American Stock Exchange.[1]

Throughout production, we worked with the panelists, and up to the end, took pains not to put words in their mouths. They have all approved the

---

[1] Reprinted with permission from 'The Economic Value of a Trading Floor: Evidence form the American Stock Exchange,' Handa, P., Schwartz, R., and Tiwari, A., Journal of Business, 2004, vol.77, no. 2, pt. 1, pp 331-355, ©2004 by The University of Chicago. All rights reserved.

final draft, and we thank them for their assistance. We also express our heartfelt thanks to the sponsors who made this conference possible (page xi). Their funding and, more importantly, endorsement of our mission, are deeply appreciated.

In my welcoming remarks at the conference, I made the following observations:

1. As of the time of this conference, three decades minus one year have passed since the landmark Securities Acts Amendments were enacted by Congress. Where are we now? The quality and intensity of the debates has remained high. As an academician, I am delighted and also a bit surprised. You would think that we would have figured it all out by now. Clearly, we have not.

2. Our markets could be in better shape. But they certainly are not static. If the objective has been to shake things up, we sure are achieving it. We are witnessing seismic change. NASDAQ has been reengineered. Eyes are now turning to the NYSE.[2]

3. A conference with the title, 'Electronic vs. Floor Based Trading,' would not be run in Europe today. The big market structure debates on the other side of the Atlantic have ended. For all intents and purposes, the issues there have already been decided.[3] Only a couple of lightly populated trading floors still remain in Europe. The major trading platforms of Europe are all electronic. Are we lagging seriously behind? Are our needs different? Do we know something that they do not? I am looking forward to hearing what some of you will say about this today.

4. 'Electronic vs. Floor Based Trading' may be a good title for the conference, but the thought is not quite right. Perhaps the question is, how effectively can electronic and floor based trading be

---

[2] During the week of April 18, 2005, about two weeks before our next Baruch Conference ('The New NASDAQ Stock Market'), two stunning announcements were made: the New York Stock Exchange would acquire Archipelago, and NASDAQ would acquire INET, a merged entity formed from Instinet's and Island's electronic communications network operations.

[3] Nevertheless, major new legislation is currently being introduced in Europe. On April 21, 2004, the European Parliament and Council introduced the Markets in Financial Instruments Directive (MiFID), which is due to take effect early in 2007. MiFID addresses a broad array of issues including the elimination of order concentration rules, the broader introduction of internalization, and the articulation of a best execution obligation.

combined? This is a big issue facing the NYSE today. Designing a pure, generic system is no longer difficult. We have learned a lot in recent years, and now have the technology to do it. On the other hand, designing an effective hybrid is a big challenge.[4] Especially when the hybrid is a fast market, slow market combination. Thoughts about this will no doubt be expressed today.

5. Public policy debates typically do not make adequate reference to cap size. For the most part, our thoughts appear to focus too much on the blue chips. However, 'one size does not fit all.' What is true for the blue chips may not be true for the mid-caps and the small-caps. The electronic trading platforms in Europe are thought to be very efficient for the European blue chips. Further market structure is needed there, however, for the mid-caps and the small-caps. The same is true on our side of the Atlantic. In our discussions, it is important not to loose sight of the smaller, less heavily traded issues.

6. Market structure issues are enormously complicated. Take the current debate over the trade-through rule.[5] Compelling reasons can be presented for keeping the rule. Compelling reasons can also be presented for eliminating it. How can we get resolution? Many of the arguments can be sorted into two groups. The first has a micro-orientation – what is good, or not good, for participants as individuals. For instance, what fits with your business plan or with my business plan? The second has a macro-orientation – what is best for all of us collectively. For instance, can we improve the quality of price discovery and quantity discovery for the broad market? Can we temper intra-day price volatility for the broad market?

---

[4] The New York Stock Exchange is currently introducing electronic, 'fast market' technology. The Big Board says that its new expanded Direct+ facility , combined with the exchange's trading floor, will turn it into a hybrid market. In fact, arguably, with its limit order book, specialist system, floor traders and upstairs market makers, the NYSE environment has historically been a hybrid marketplace.

[5] On Thursday, June 9, 2005, Regulation NMS (Reg NMS) was formally adopted by the Securities and Exchange Commission (SEC). In so doing, the Commission imposed a trade-through rule that included top of the book protection of limit orders. The trade-through rule was also extended to the NASDAQ market (the trade-through prohibition had formerly applied to the exchange market only).

Personally, I put more weight on the macro-view. Bill Donaldson made an interesting request for the 'macro' approach at the April 21 SEC Reg NMS hearings in New York: 'Try,' he said, 'to put aside your institutional interests, your biases and even your current business models... and instead give us the benefit of your frank insights about how the proposals, and the alternatives to the proposals, will serve our capital markets and the investing public.'[6] Do you think we will be able to do this today?

7. History will show that, today, the industry is at a tipping point. The uses to which we are putting technology are changing rapidly and, with Reg NMS, our regulatory framework is once again shifting. How will this all play out?

I then said to the audience, 'Let's jump into the heart of the issue and get going with an exciting day.'

Robert A. Schwartz

---

[6] Securities Industry News, pp 1 and 20, April 26, 2004.

Chapter 1: GETTING THE TRADES MADE

Moderator –Avner Wolf, Zicklin School of Business, Baruch College
Chairman, Economics & Finance Department and Director, International Programs

Puneet Handa, University of Iowa
Associate Professor

Michael Pagano, Villanova University
Assistant Professor

James Ross, Burlington Capital Markets
Managing Director, Call Market Trading

AVNER WOLF: Good morning, everyone. Welcome to this beautiful vertical campus at Baruch College.

Before I hand over the microphone to Mike, Puneet and Jim, I would like to mention some work involving Bob and I that is related to the presentations that will be made on this panel by Mike and Puneet. In one of our papers, we found that traditional buyers and sellers are commonly in the market together at the same time. An important reason is that they have different views about the stocks they are trading. At this same moment in time, some participants are bulls and some are bears. Some want to buy, while others want to sell. You will see a connection between this reality and Mike Pagano's discussion about book building. Mike's paper, which is being produced with Bob and Archishman Chakraborty, shows how hard it is to get orders out of traders' pockets and onto the books even when some of the big participants are seeking to buy at the same time as others are looking to sell.

In another paper that Bob and I are involved in, we develop a model of price discovery that follows a new, reasonably realistic, and rather unorthodox approach. The paper is based on the assumption that market participants have divergent valuations (again, some are bulls and some are bears) for a security. We show how a divergence of expectations translates in the real world into price discovery being a complex, dynamic process. This view of reality ties in with the discussion that we will be hearing from Puneet about the timing of order placement. Puneet and his co-authors, Bob and Ashish Tiwari, find that floor broker-timed order handling generally lowers execution costs.

Lastly, Jim Ross will talk about these issues from the point of view of a market architect who, as a practitioner, has seen in action what Mike, Puneet, and their co-authors have modeled in theory.

I invite Mike to speak first.

MICHAEL PAGANO: Thanks, Avner. My paper, which is a joint work with Archishman Chakraborty and Bob Schwartz, is titled 'Traders' Dilemma.' We consider how traders enter their orders into a market and build a book. We all know that large, institutional traders typically hold their orders back – in whole or in part – in an attempt to protect themselves from adverse price impact. But holding back results in undesirable outcomes. We talk, for instance, about slicing and dicing, delayed executions and latent liquidity. Ultimately, holding orders back results in markets being less liquid. Our paper models this dynamic. Through a better understanding of it, we hope to gain insights that will lead to the development of more efficient trading mechanisms. In a nutshell, a mechanism is more efficient if it enables large participants to step forward more readily with their orders and trade.

You may have seen the movie, A Beautiful Mind, starring Russell Crowe. Crowe played the role of John Nash, the brilliant economist/mathematician who won a Nobel Prize for having developed non-cooperative game theory. His contribution to game theory – the Nash equilibrium – was a significant effort at demonstrating what happens when 'most desirable outcomes' are sought by players in non-cooperative games. In this Nash equilibrium, no player can gain an advantage by unilaterally changing his strategy if the other players do not change their strategies at the same time. Nash's basic insight was that when people compete, they do not necessarily achieve the most desirable results that would be obtained if they instead cooperated. We recognize this behavior in the context of the equity markets and formally model it. Our objective is to obtain, using a game theory structure, a crisper, more formal understanding of the dynamics of the book building process.

Our conclusions are not based on any assumption of investor irrationality. They are based on the very rational idea that every trader is out for his or her own self-interest. Nevertheless, at the end of the day, each participant does wind up with an undesirable outcome. Recognizing this, we suggest that there is a role for a financial intermediary to play. The role, in our terminology, is that of an 'animator' who facilitates the book building process.

Here is a quick primer on game theory. John Nash applied his classic idea, the Nash equilibrium, to a game known as the Prisoners' Dilemma (Exhibit 1).

The Prisoners' Dilemma
(A Nash Equilibrium)

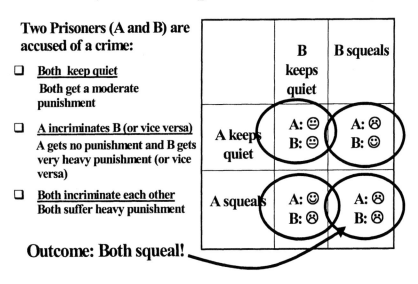

Two Prisoners (A and B) are accused of a crime:

❑ <u>Both keep quiet</u>
   Both get a moderate punishment

❑ <u>A incriminates B (or vice versa)</u>
   A gets no punishment and B gets very heavy punishment (or vice versa)

❑ <u>Both incriminate each other</u>
   Both suffer heavy punishment

Outcome: Both squeal!

	B keeps quiet	B squeals
A keeps quiet	A: 😐 B: 😐	A: ☹ B: 🙂
A squeals	A: 🙂 B: ☹	A: ☹ B: ☹

Exhibit 1. The Prisoners' Dilemma

Assume that two prisoners, prisoner A and prisoner B, have both been accused of a serious crime, and that they are being interrogated in separate cells. Neither knows what the other has or may reveal. They are found guilty (or not) and are punished (or not) depending on what each of them says when interrogated. The alternatives, for each, are either to keep quiet or to squeal and incriminate the other. If they both keep quiet, instead of facing a very serious charge like the death penalty, they would get off with only a minor charge. As they would both be relatively satisfied with that outcome, that outcome for both of them is the best solution in this game.

Now for the dilemma. Both prisoners have an incentive to deviate from the 'do not confess' option. Each will fair better by squealing and incriminating the other if the other one keeps quiet. In this situation, the 'squealer' (say prisoner A) gets no punishment and can walk free, while the other prisoner (B) receives a very serious punishment. So A has an incentive to incriminate B. For the same reason, B has an incentive to squeal on A so that he can go free. The bottom line is that both are incented to incriminate the other, even though both would be better off if they both kept quiet. Consequently, both squeal. The two prisoners wind up with heavy sentences and are in a worse situation than if they had cooperated (instead of having competed) with each other.

We can bring this idea of the Nash equilibrium into the world of trading (Exhibit2).

The Traders' Dilemma
(A Variation on Prisoners' Dilemma)

Two large traders: A is trying to buy, and B is trying to sell, a large block

❏ **A & B disclose at opening call**
  Both trade with no market impact

❏ **A or B does not enter opening call**
  A subsequently trades at a better price and B gets very inferior execution, or vice versa

❏ **A & B do not enter opening call**
  Both subsequently get inferior executions

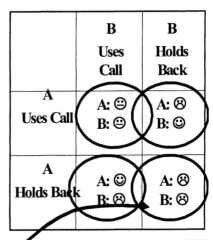

	B Uses Call	B Holds Back
A Uses Call	A: 😊 B: 😊	A: ☹ B: 🙂
A Holds Back	A: 🙂 B: ☹	A: ☹ B: ☹

Outcome: Both hold their orders back to their mutual detriment and the book does not build

Exhibit 2. The Traders' Dilemma

Consider the situation where there are two large traders with large orders to execute. Let each trader know that the other is out there, but neither knows when the other will show up. Let trader A be looking to buy a large block of stock at the same time that trader B is looking to sell a large block of stock. The question for both of them is: Should they enter their orders at a morning call auction or go to the market after the morning call?

We show that trader A and trader B will both hold their orders back from the call. The reason is the same as it is for the prisoners' dilemma. Here, we call it the 'traders' dilemma.' Comparable to what we showed for the prisoners' dilemma, the optimal outcome for both would be for both to go to the opening call. In this case, the two would meet and provide liquidity to each other. In so doing, they would both happily receive an execution with little or no market impact.

But, just as is the case with the prisoners' dilemma, both traders have an incentive to deviate from the mutually beneficial strategy. Trader A will say, 'It makes sense for me to hold my buy order back and to wait for trader B to sell and push down the price. By being patient, I will be able to buy at a lower price. The same logic holds for trader B: wait for A to come in, for A to buy, push the price up, and then to sell at a higher price. For each of them, holding back (which is equivalent to not telling the truth) while the other places an order in the call leads to an excellent result. On the other hand, not holding back when the other does and going into the call alone leads to a bad result.

Consequently, as with the prisoners' dilemma, they both do that which is undesirable for both of them collectively – they both hold back from the opening call. The result? Both traders go to a market that is less liquid and wind up paying for their decisions in terms of higher market impact costs. Nevertheless, A's behavior is not irrational, and neither is B's. Each is basically following a self-interested, self-optimizing trading strategy given his or her expectations of what the other will do. But the outcome of their strategies is that book building is difficult.

What can we do about it? From the point of view of market design, how can we change a market's structure to avoid the undesirable Nash equilibrium? We focus on one solution in particular. We believe that an intermediary – an entity like a direct access broker, the classic exchange specialist, or an upstairs market maker – should (and does) take an active role in the book building process. We see the intermediary as a facilitator who animates the market. The animation process may involve providing capital, not to supply liquidity per se, but to get big buyers and sellers to step forward in a way that enables them to supply liquidity to each other.

On behalf of my co-authors Archishman and Bob, along with John Nash and Russell Crowe, I thank you.

WOLF: Thanks to you, Mike. Puneet?

PUNEET HANDA: I will talk about a paper that I wrote with Bob and Ashish Tiwari, 'The Economic Value of a Trading Floor: Evidence from the American Stock Exchange,' published in the April issue of the Journal of Business.[7] We had some interesting results that I would like to share with you.

We looked at the American Stock Exchange (Amex) and asked ourselves, 'Does the floor have any economic value?' All around the world, we are seeing a move to electronic exchanges. The question is, is the traditional trading floor archaic? Is it time to close the floor down? Is it there only because it has always been there? Or does the floor have economic value?

We did our analysis using 2001 data, focusing on the American Stock Exchange. The Amex receives orders in two ways. Some orders (floor orders) come from the floor brokers, and some orders (system orders) come in over the Amex's electronic order delivery system. We compared the execution costs of the floor and system orders. The floor brokers, of course, incur handling costs. The question is: Does their superior order handling save enough in execution costs to justify the handling costs? We conjecture that this is the case, but it is not something that we are able to show or to prove. Rather, we focus more modestly on whether or not floor brokers have a gross value added, on whether or not the shares that they handle incur lower execution costs.

We originally started our study with Amex data for October 1996. But by the time the paper was finished and got reviewed by the Journal of Business, the referee said, 'Good job, but the data are too old. Please redo the tests.' So we went back to the Amex and they provided us with data for 973 stocks for October of 2001. We retested everything with the new data. The results confirmed what we had previously found with the 1996 data. Thus, we have further confidence that our findings are robust.

Information about the share volume and number of trades, trade sizes, etcetera, are given in Exhibit 3.

Descriptive Statistics

	Share Volume	No. of Trades	Trade Size	Trade Time
Floor	110,489,600	49,940	2,212.45	26.64
PER	361,739,540	388,194	931.85	27.87
All Trades	472,229,140	438,134	1077.82	27.73

Exhibit 3. Descriptive Statistics

We examined over 472 million shares traded, of which roughly 110 million came from the floor. That is, roughly, over 23%. We examined over 438 thousand trades of which roughly 10% (49,940) were floor based. Floor trades account for over 23% total share volume but only 10% of the trades because the floor trade size is much bigger (2,212 shares) as opposed to the PER trade size (932 shares). Trade time reflects the time, on average, for 31 trades to occur (for each trade, we examine the 15 trades that precede it and the 15 trades that follow it).

Our research design is as follows. We classified each trade according to the order that triggered it. For instance, a trade triggered by a floor order to buy is classified as a 'buy trade' and as a 'floor trade.' In total, we considered four combinations of floor vs. system orders and buy vs. sell orders. For both buy and sell trades, we matched the sample of floor trades to a sample of non-floor trades. Trades had to be in the same stock; in the same direction (buy or sell); the execution price of the PER trade had to be within 20% of the price of the floor trade; and, finally, the size of the PER trade had to be within 20% of the size of the floor trade. While satisfying these conditions, we were able to match 48,471 floor trades (which was 97.06 percent of our sample). We compared each matched trade in terms of the quoted half-spread, the effective half-spread, and the realized half-spread. The quoted half-spread is the spread (divided by 2) that you would measure when simply selling at the bid and buying at the offer (which is not very realistic). The effective half-spread is the difference between the price at which your order has executed and the mid-point of the quoted spread at the time of your trade. It is a reasonably good measure except that sometimes transaction prices move because of 'permanent' price changes. To get rid of that permanent change, we used the realized half-spread. The realized half-spread reflects the difference between a trade price and the mid-point of the bid-ask spread 15 trades later.

Values for the three spread measures are shown in Exhibit 4.

Matched Pair Results

(in *bps*)	Q ½ Spread	E ½ Spread	R ½ Spread
Floor	16.23	8.11	-3.06
PER	17.47	10.27	4.43
Difference	-1.24 **	2.16 **	-7.49 **

**Significant at the 1% level.

Exhibit 4. Matched Pair Results

The quoted half-spread for the floor trades averaged 16.23, and for electronic trading it is 17.47, a difference of -1.24. The difference is statistically significant. The floor brokers did better than the electronic trades by 1.24 basis points. The comparable values for the effective half-spread are 8.11 for the floor trades and 10.27 for the system trades, a difference of -2.16 basis points. Again, the difference is statistically significant. Finally, look at the realized half-spread. This measure is the most important, realistic, and appropriate of the three. Overall, trades handled by floor brokers have a significantly smaller realized half-spread than do PER trades (-3.06 bps vs. 4.43 bps), a difference of 7.49 bps. This is a statistically significant victory for the floor. Notice that the realized half-spread for the floor trades is actually a negative 3.06. What does it mean for it to be negative? It means that the floor delivered order was executed when the market was moving up for a buy order (or when the market was moving down for a sell order). If the market continued to move up (after a purchase) or down (after a sale), the order was turned into a trade at the strategically right time. It is the effective timing of the floor trades that resulted in the realized half-spreads, on average, being negative.

We performed some further econometric analyses, and I will give you a brief overview of the results. We found that larger orders were more likely to execute on the floor. We looked at a market imbalance variable (the imbalance between buy and sell orders), and the coefficient told us that, as market imbalance increases, floor trades are more likely to occur. Specifically, a floor trader is more apt to step forward and execute an order when the book thickens on the side of the market (buy or sell) that the order is on. Further, when price has moved up prior to an actual trade, a floor trader is less apt to step forth with a buy order. Similarly, if price has moved down, a floor trader is less apt to step forward and execute a sell order. In other words, following a price change, you do not get as many floor orders. You tend to get system orders instead. We also looked at the time of day. Floor trades are more likely (relative to system trades) in the morning and in the late afternoon at the approach of the close. Finally, we found that floor trades are more likely for low volume stocks. That is, the mid-caps and the small-caps are more likely to be traded on the floor.

Here are the major conclusions presented in the paper:

1. Trades handled by floor brokers have significantly lower execution costs. I know this will shake up some people, but it is a fact.
2. The floor trading mechanism is preferred for larger size trades, on occasions when the book is thick on the side of the order initiating the trade, but not following a recent price change. The floor trading

mechanism is also preferred after the start of trading, near the market close, and for less liquid stocks.

3. The Amex trading floor has economic value. In fact, we measured this economic value based on our estimates. The Amex trading floor resulted in a total savings of $4.36 million in the month of October 2001. That is our estimate of the amount of gross value that the floor added.

4. Floor traders exhibit strategic behavior. They become more aggressive in response to a thickening of the book on their side of the market, and they become more patient following large price changes that, if chased, could result in costly executions. In contrast, system orders are more apt to chase recent price changes.

WOLF: Interesting, indeed. Thank you, Puneet. Jim, please. It is time to hear from a practitioner.

JAMES ROSS: I must say that it is interesting for me to be on this panel with the professors. I figure, in the infinite wisdom of Bob Schwartz, that he is taking the opportunity to juxtapose the practical against the academic.

Most of my career has been in the crossing area, and I am still trying to understand Bob Schwartz's 1986 paper on call auction trading. As Bob has pointed out, for the past 15 to 20 years, we have been implementing new technologies. So, where are we today? What have we actually implemented? We are still having issues of volatility. We are still having issues with finding size. In many ways, things have gotten worse, even as we have seen heightened competition between the various ECNs and now between the New York Stock Exchange and the various ECNs.

A couple of years ago, Bob put up a slide on the first half-hour of trading in Cisco.[8] That slide showed that, if you count the number of trades that occurred in the first half-hour of trading (almost 10,000 trades that went up in the first 30 minutes), and then divide the number of trades by 1,800 seconds, you see a whole host of trades (over five) going up in any given second. Using an admittedly unscientific approach, I looked at the first half-hour of trading for Cisco yesterday. 14,000 trades went up in the first 30 minutes (7.8 trades per second), for about nine million shares, and with an average trade size of 600 shares.

---

[8] The data on the first half-hour of trading for Cisco are for January 22, 2001. They are presented in Robert Schwartz and Reto Francioni, Equity Markets in Action: The Fundamentals of Liquidity, Market Structure and Trading, John Wiley & Sons, 2004, page 133.

With technology, we have made everything far more efficient. We have reaped a lot of the benefits of that efficiency. It has helped us to lower costs, generally across the board. But at the same time, we are still plagued with some real big issues about getting size done and about dealing with volatility. As we go forward, we need to consider the use of time. Now that we are in a decimalized, sub-second environment, we need to get back to reality. We must look at the basic model that we are operating our market structure on. It is not so much about the speed of getting there, but what is happening with the orders once they are there.

One of the things that I have always liked about the call auction trading concept is that it is a different kind of animal compared to the continuous market. The call provides some interesting dynamics in contrast to a continuous market. I stress that the call is not a replacement for continuous trading. Some people feel that there is this desire just to take the liquidity, run an auction, and be done with it. I do not agree.

There are obvious benefits to aggregating liquidity at specific moments in time by running an auction at the open and another one at the close. If you look at the issues between electronic trading and floor trading, you realize that the centralization of orders is good. Whether you do it by connectivity in the ECN environment, or you do it by saying that you have to be at this or that particular place, there is a great benefit to getting orders together so that the orders can find each other. Taking this one step further, benefits are realized when you aggregate orders at specific, pre-determined moments in time. That is what crossing does.

I joined Instinet in the late '80s, a time when ITG and Instinet were both developing their crosses. It was really tough getting institutions to start using the crossing systems. It was not even a question of getting them to be at a place where they would trade – it was difficult just getting them to start considering it.

Nevertheless, the investing institutions in the late '80s and early '90s were very supportive of new ways of doing things. They were much more willing to try new ideas, to innovate, and even to support a new system. That obviously helped Instinet and ITG. Through the 90's, we had a rash of innovations that came and went with varying degrees of success. Some of them were ahead of their time. Now I wonder if institutions are just overwhelmed with the technology and the past innovations. Right now, they just want to deal with growing their businesses. They do not have much of a desire to take on yet another new model. But we need the institutions to support innovation. We haven't actually had a lot lately except for the advent of NASDAQ's auction and Archipelago's auction.

The spirit of innovation is going to be critical to the evolution of the markets.

WOLF: Thank you, Jim. You have given us more food for thought. Now it is time to open this up for discussion. Are there any questions from the audience?

UNIDENTIFIED SPEAKER [From the Floor]: I would like to know how the prisoners' dilemma applies to the setting where you have more than two players. In reality, there are many buyers and many sellers, but in the prisoners' dilemma you have only two, like a duopoly.

PAGANO: What we showed you here is a Reader's Digest version of the paper and the model behind it. The analysis generalizes to multiple players. You can think of it as many large buyers and many large sellers, and they know they can possibly move the market with their big orders, so they are going to hold back. It really does not matter if it is one person or 2,000 people in that kind of a situation.

WOLF: Puneet, did you address accentuated volatility in your paper?

HANDA: No.

WOLF: You did not address it at all?

HANDA: No.

WOLF: Okay. Thank you.

PAUL DAVIS (TIAA-CREF) [From the Floor]: I have a question for Puneet. Commissions tend to be a lot more expensive when you give the order to a broker who then gives it to the floor. It is roughly a five to one ratio. Let's say that the commission when you trade on the floor would be a nickel a share, versus trading electronically at a penny a share. That is four cents a share of savings, which, for 100,000,000 shares, is roughly $4 million. So it looks like the value-added for the people doing the trading has just gone away. Could you address that issue? What happens when you take commissions into account?

HANDA: The way we looked at it, for larger orders, it could be economical to go to the floor. For smaller orders it may not be because of the commissions, because of the order handling costs.

SCHWARTZ [From the Floor]: Let me add to that. We are asserting that there is value in the discretionary handling of orders. Whether that value is enough to justify the costs is an issue that I would not begin to touch. But what you are saying, Paul, is that, on average, the incremental benefits and costs are quite similar. Isn't it interesting how markets can equilibrate? It means that traders know when to go to the floor and when not to go. For some of the trades, the value added by the floor is probably more than the incremental commission costs, and for others trades the value added is less. Does that help, Paul?

DAVIS: Yes.

ERIC BARRET (CIBC) [From the Floor]: October 2001 data might be outdated due to new algorithmic trading tools and smart order routing tools provided by the direct access providers. Have you taken that into account in maybe a newer study?

HANDA: No, right now we have not. We would like to if we can get the data from the Amex. Things keep changing and one could certainly update the study.

WOLF: Jim, you wanted to make a comment?

ROSS: Yes. In Mike's prisoners' dilemma, two institutions are trying to find each other. What is critical in book building is that it is not always just two big institutions with two large orders. A lot of times − and I have certainly found this in my crossing experiences − you have an index arb guy versus a large active manager, or it could be a quantitative trader against a specialist, or it could be a market maker who is reducing risk versus an indexer. There is a tendency with each of today's electronic matching systems to cater to a particular constituency. These systems, which include Liquidnet and ITG, either exclude broker dealers outright or else through prohibitive pricing. Also, these systems sometimes focus on a select group of institutions, which have OMS technologies or specific investment strategies. I firmly believe that we now need new electronic matching systems, which are more inclusive of the various constituencies, from the buy-side to the sell-side. We need systems that respond to active and passive strategies in small-cap through large cap stocks.

One of the critical aspects of building a good, broad book is getting multiple parties with different trading horizons and different investment strategies to participate. It is a win/win situation when you can bring together someone committing capital and someone who is investing, and have them both get a trade off where they both feel that they have benefited. Maybe one has a short-term strategy and one has a longer-term strategy. This gets back to the structure of the system, and to how it permits many people with divergent trading strategies to come together and find each other. Unfortunately, it seems that the market structure that we have sometimes forces people apart as they adjust their strategies to get the results that they are ultimately looking for.

ROBERT WOOD (University of Memphis) [From the Floor]: I am curious about the realized spreads and about how the floor brokers are able to systematically have a negative realized spread. In essence, this means either that they are able to time their trades extremely well, or that they are trading systematically with uninformed traders. Could you comment on that?

HANDA: We believe that they are able to time their trades well. Now, a negative average does not mean that every number is negative. I mean, overwhelmingly large realized spreads are negative. So they are (on average) executing when the price is moving in an upward direction for a buy, or in a downward direction for a sell. Hence, the floor brokers are able to time their executions extremely well. The floor brokers are sitting there, watching the way things are going. If the book thickens on their side of the market and the price starts to move, that is when they trade.

WOOD: I worry about the extent to which the floor is about doing favors. I have heard a situation described where you have a good floor broker, you want to buy 50,000 shares of GE, and the floor broker 'knows' that someone is working off an order of 300,000 shares. So your broker waits until that is done and then gets you a better price. In essence, you cannot do a favor for one person without hurting somebody else. If that was my 300,000-share order, I would say that you were fading my order – you were fading the market ahead of it. If you can do that systematically, you are going to be able to get, on average, a negative realized spread. You cannot do a favor for one person without hurting somebody else on the floor. Comments?

HANDA: That is a possibility. We did not have a chance to investigate that kind of a thing with our data, but it is an alternative explanation of what may be going on.

SCHWARTZ [From the Floor]: Perhaps our paper should come with a surgeon general's warning that it should be read properly and in context. When you examine a large body of data like this, you see that the floor brokers are responding to signals that we can capture. We have captured two major signals – the imbalance that is on the book and market direction. We have not captured knowledge that there is a big order in somebody's pocket. We only know about the orders that are on the book.

If I want to buy and there are a lot of buy orders on the book and the sells have thinned out, I do not wait to be a liquidity provider. Instead, I move forward and execute. We are finding very significant responses to variables that we can measure. When we see the positive correlations that we get, and when we see the contrasts, I think it is insightful. It suggests that the floor brokers are doing something of positive value. They are timing their orders. We can discuss further whether this justifies all of the costs, as Paul Davis just pointed out, and whether there are other things going on. But it is nice to see some evidence that there are positives as well.

My last comment is, hey, we are academicians. This is an academic institution. We are like Fox News, fair and balanced.

WOLF: I'm sorry we have to end this session. I would like to thank the panel for their presentations and discussion, and move on to the next session.

CHAPTER 2: INCREASING RETURNS BY DECREASING TRADING COSTS

Edward J. Nicoll

Chief Executive Officer, Instinet Group Incorporated

Thank you for the invitation to join you today to discuss some of the most critical market structure issues facing our industry. I cannot think of a more important public policy issue facing all of us than how we design and shape the regulatory regime governing the trading of listed securities. For over three decades, we've operated under a set of rules and regulations constructed before electronic markets existed as competitive alternatives. Consequently, those of us in that business have long argued for finding a fair and effective way to integrate electronic markets into this regulatory environment. To its credit, the U.S. Securities and Exchange Commission has been a leading advocate in addressing these issues. Recently, the SEC issued its proposed rule, and has reached out to many of us to offer our thoughts and recommendations. Those of you who know me could guess that I was pretty eager to join that debate.

In recent appearances before both the SEC and the U.S. Congress, I've sat beside my competitors from the NYSE and listened closely to their arguments. Today, I'd like to examine some of their arguments and offer my thoughts on the assumptions underlying their case.

Proponents of the existing trade-through rule insist that the SEC's proposed reform of the rule will result in investor confusion, weakened markets and perhaps unscrupulous broker conduct. Pretty serious stuff. Yet contrary to this rhetoric, actual experience tells a different story – a story of investor benefits. Indeed, we have been conducting an experiment for many years now that allows us to compare the NASDAQ market, personified by multiple competing electronic marketplaces with no trade-through rule, and the NYSE market, personified by one central pool of liquidity and a trade-through rule. By comparing these two markets, we can learn a lot. I believe that the record shows that the NASDAQ market performs better, especially for larger securities. The NASDAQ market has also clearly fostered greater competition and innovation than the NYSE market that is essentially unchanged for the past 25 years since the introduction of the National Market System. Just look at the array of front-ends and order routing technologies that have sprung up from multiple ECNs along with technology vendors such as Lava, compared to the listed environment. Let's look at some facts.

The SEC's 11Ac1-5 statistics show that the NASDAQ market actually has LOWER effective spreads than the NYSE market in S&P 500 stocks. This means that investors pay less in transaction costs on NASDAQ stocks than NYSE stocks.

One example is a simple comparison of two similar securities, Microsoft and GE. Both trade in nearly the same price range, both have the same market capitalization and a similar number of shares outstanding. Yet, during the month of March, the average time weighted bid or ask size was approximately 26,000 shares in Microsoft as compared to approximately 13,000 shares in GE. In short, Microsoft had approximately double the size at the inside quote. And it's not like the quote was wider in Microsoft. In fact, the average time weighted quoted spread was 7 tenths of a penny in Microsoft as compared to 1.6 cents in GE. In this case, NASDAQ performed twice as well.

If that is not enough, let's look at slippage. Slippage, for those who are not familiar with the term, is the difference between the displayed price at the time the order is entered versus the execution price actually received. Therefore, slippage is in some ways a measure of liquidity and the accuracy of displayed quotations. Instinet SmartRouter routes millions of shares to the NYSE and to NASDAQ, oftentimes at the same time for program traders. For the entire month of February, we found that the average slippage in NYSE stocks is approximately 2.5 times greater than in NASDAQ stocks. The fact that we see less slippage in NASDAQ stocks may suggest that there is GREATER liquidity in NASDAQ stocks than in NYSE stocks.

We are lucky that we have statistics available as to how a market without a trade-through rule operates. Policy decisions should not be based on rhetoric, but on facts. And in this case, the facts are available. Moreover,

I urge firms to make additional information publicly available about their internal statistics regarding the amount of slippage they see when trading NASDAQ stocks versus New York Stocks or any other fact they think is relevant. I believe the results will surprise many people who simply assume the NYSE market is superior. While that may have been true a few years ago, it is no longer true today.

The statistics that I have cited today reflect benefits that are more than theoretical. A narrower spread saves investors money by lowering transaction costs. Greater size at the inside and narrower spreads throw cold water on the assertion that a trade-through rule is necessary to encourage limit orders. It is not. Transparency and access are sufficient.

Not only have investors benefited from uninhibited competition when trading NASDAQ securities, but due to the mere POSSIBILITY of trade-throughs being permitted, investors will soon see benefits in the NYSE market. I am referring to the fact that the SEC's consideration of allowing market participants to trade-through 'slow' markets caused the NYSE to suddenly announce that it intends to make improvements to Direct+.

No wonder people may want to trade-through markets like the NYSE. Contrary to the rhetoric, the SEC execution quality statistics show that an investor sending an order to the NYSE is equally likely to receive a worse price relative to the NYSE quote than a better price. And if the market is volatile, I am sure that market participants will tell you that the likelihood of price dis-improvement increases significantly.

Despite what I believe is clear proof that investors benefit from the lower spreads and greater competition that result from not having a trade-through rule for NASDAQ stocks, many still have reservations about eliminating the trade-through rule or even having an effective opt-out provision. The first reservation is that the elimination of the trade-through rule or the adoption of an effective opt-out provision will allow unscrupulous brokers to give their customers inferior executions. This concern, however, does not adequately consider the broker's duty of best execution. Any broker who simply begins executing orders at other than the best available price will likely find himself facing regulatory action. SRO's like NASD Regulation can easily detect trade-throughs and bring regulatory actions when necessary. But in reality, as reflected in NASDAQ today, even in the absence of a trade-through rule, most retail customers will not trade-through. I am not aware of a best execution problem in NASDAQ stocks. This is because, as a business and regulatory necessity, brokers with retail customers make certain that all retail customers are executed at the best-displayed price when trading NASDAQ stocks. The fact that many retail brokers receive more investor orders in NASDAQ stocks than NYSE stocks indicates that the NASDAQ environment has worked well and that the duty of best execution is sufficient to ensure that retail customers get the best price.

The second reservation is one that was discussed time and again at the SEC hearing a few weeks ago. It is the claim that permitting trade-throughs will simply allow sophisticated investors and institutions to ignore the limit orders of retail investors. And when they see their orders traded through, these investors will lose confidence in the market and post fewer limit orders. I call this the 'sanctity of limit orders argument.'

I made the point at the recent SEC hearing and I want to reiterate it here today. If all the people who argue that we need trade-through rules to protect the sanctity of limit orders really believed their argument, then they would be lobbying for a mandatory price and time priority rule. But they are not.

To see why they are not, let's compare a price priority regime to a time/price priority regime. Let's say a retail investor posts the best bid of $20. In a price priority regime (a regime with a trade-through prohibition), nobody could trade at a price LESS THAN $20 without first executing the $20 bid. But because there is no time priority but only price priority, other market participants can trade at the SAME price as the $20 bid without executing against the $20 bid. Note the harm to the customer. The customer posts the best price in the marketplace and watches as everyone else free rides off his $20 bid while he fails to receive an execution. We can call this PRICE MATCHING. In a TIME-price priority regime, price matching cannot happen. Nobody could execute an order at $20 until they traded with the customer who first posted the $20 bid.

If people were really concerned about the sanctity of limit orders, they would support TIME AND PRICE priority between markets rather than simply price priority. Time and price priority between markets would eliminate price-matching behavior. Note that price matching occurs MUCH more frequently than trade-throughs and, therefore harms customers much more than trade-throughs that, as we know from our experience with NASDAQ, are a relatively rare occurrence. Even though price matching is much more common and harms the customer the same way as trade-throughs, you do not hear anyone demanding an end to price matching.

Why? Because price matching is the business model of many of the intermediated markets. In both specialist-based markets and market maker-based markets, price matching is a basic component of their business model. That is one reason why I found the arguments at the hearing so ironic. Some of the biggest proponents of the sanctity of limit order argument were also the biggest price matchers. I believe it is disingenuous to talk about the sanctity of limit orders and then support price matching.

Before you start thinking that I am advocating a mandatory time-price priority rule, I better make it clear that I am completely opposed to any type of inter-market priority rules—be it price priority or time-price priority. But I do believe there are two legitimate viewpoints in the debate over market structure and priority rules.

Either you favor strict time-price priority that effectively would lead to one marketplace, or you favor a market with transparency and access but no mandates as to where orders should be sent – which is my view. I favor a free market, one that looks exactly like NASDAQ does today, because I believe the benefits of competition between marketplaces far outweigh the theoretical benefits of centralizing all order flow in one marketplace. As I noted earlier, the statistics show that the NASDAQ market is superior in a number of stocks despite the fact that trading is spread among numerous venues, while NYSE trading is centralized on one venue.

I also believe that with competing marketplaces, there will be more innovation, lower prices, better services, and, most importantly, better price discovery. By mandating price-time priority, we would be saying that we know that the best market structure is a price-time priority model and that we won't permit any other market types. I think that is a mistake - we still have much to learn about what makes the most efficient market. To adapt just one type of market structure because economists tell us that it is the best is risky. After all, we already know that economists have predicted 9 out of the last 5 recessions.

I believe that a trade-through rule, a rule that permits price matching but does not at least have an effective opt-out provision, is the kind of compromise that ends up harming investors. On the one hand, it fails to protect limit orders in any significant way because it allows price matching. And on the other hand, the priority rules virtually eliminate intermarket competition by forcing operational and technical uniformity on each marketplace, negating price competition, system performance differences, or any other differentiating features markets may develop.

Priority rules are not necessary because I do not believe you need a rule to compel market participants to access the best price. Market participants will access the best price if they believe it is truly accessible.

Period. And any effort to define 'fast' or 'slow' is an exercise in substituting the government's judgment of what is 'fast enough' for a particular marketplace.

Interestingly enough, a common misperception is that the market is already too fast and that milliseconds may not matter to investors. In fact milliseconds do benefit investors. The reason that NASDAQ spreads are narrower than those on the NYSE is because milliseconds allow market participants to narrow spreads. Milliseconds, which translate to the ability to control risk, allow market participants who provide liquidity to narrow the spreads for all investors. The faster liquidity providers can put in an order, cancel an order, or update an order, the more liquidity they can put into the marketplace and the narrower they can make the spread and still be profitable. If it takes 10 seconds to cancel an order, by definition you have to put in a less aggressive limit order. So making the market as fast as possible benefits almost everyone. Everyone, that is, except intermediaries who believe that they will be less profitable when spreads are narrower. No wonder they want to slow things down.

For those who worry that a lack of a trade-through rule will discourage limit orders but aren't swayed by my earlier statistics, let's look at another example. Within the NASDAQ market, ECNs emerged from a nearly zero market share in 1996, to a dominant portion of the price discovery today. When we talk about ECNs today, we are really talking about an electronic marketplace – so the term really should include INET, ARCA, and SuperMontage. These 3 markets only display limit orders. If the people advancing the sanctity of limit orders arguments were right, none of these electronic markets would be successful. Why? Because there is no trade-through rule that requires market participants to interact with their quotes. The way some people describe it, those limit orders would sit there in perpetuity due to the lack of a trade-through rule. In fact, it is a wonder anyone posts a limit order in NASDAQ. Which I suppose makes it a verifiable miracle that NASDAQ has lower effective spreads than the NYSE in S&P 500 Stocks.

In summary, I believe that the experiences on the NASDAQ market versus the NYSE market show that a trade-through rule inhibits competition and actually harms rather than benefits investors. I also believe that in making this policy decision, we must use the available statistics that allow us to compare the NYSE and NASDAQ markets.

We are in the closing weeks of this robust and at times heated debate over market structure. While I will not venture a guess about how it will all turn out, I do remain an optimist. More than anything else, I remain optimistic that competitive solutions will eventually triumph over monopolistic practices. Thank you. I would be happy to answer some questions.

ROBERT WOOD (University of Memphis) [From the Floor]: Ed, I share your view of the tremendous competition that we are seeing on NASDAQ between the ECNs. I resonate to your idea of 'let the free market preside.' But I am confused about why the ECNs are not gaining traction with listed shares compared to how they have on NASDAQ. For example, ArcaEx reportedly experiences hundreds of trade-throughs a day as the New York specialist is ignoring a better quote on Arca. How do you reconcile that with the idea that ignoring the trade-through leads to better competition?

NICOLL: I am not here to bash the NYSE. Maybe they are right, maybe there is something magic that goes on down there on the floor that I do not understand. Maybe it is correct to give a privileged position to one dealer in perpetuity, and then allow everybody else to trade around him on the floor. Maybe that is a better model. All that we are asking is that the competition be allowed to play out between the different models in a fair way.

Agency markets, by definition, have no control over their quotes because their quotes are always a function of the orders that are placed by their customers. When you have transparent agency markets competing against a market that has manual intervention in the quote, and you have a trade-through rule that permits the disabling of one market by another, then the one that can be manipulated (I am not saying that they have manipulated it) has a stated advantage over the one that cannot be manipulated. We do not price match. We cannot. Otherwise we could not be a pure agency marketplace.

My argument is simple. Competition between these different market models ought to be allowed to play out freely. If the NYSE's vaunted floor provides better liquidity, then so be it. We were down at the SEC before anybody else, before any reporter ever printed the words 'trade-through.' We talked to the Commission about how the trade-through rule does not allow us to compete fairly with the New York Stock Exchange. It is the trade-through rule that prevents Arca from gaining market share from the NYSE. Market share is liquidity. Market share is by far the single most important product that any market can deliver.

The New York Stock Exchange's liquidity pool is an enormous asset, and they should be able to defend it. It would be amazing if they were to lose that liquidity pool. The most important thing that a buyer or a seller wants is a place that has lots of other buyers and sellers. It is not surprising to me that the NYSE has been a tough competitor. They have an enormous amount of liquidity that is arguably the result of over 200 years of custom and culture. Their liquidity is also the result of protective regulations. If the trade-through rule is not such a powerful protector of that market share, then why the heck is the New York Stock Exchange hanging on to it like grim death? Why do not they let competition play out?

JAMES ANGEL (Georgetown University) [From the Floor]: One of the other mistaken but well-intentioned proposals in Reg NMS is to put a price control on the fees that trading platforms can charge. This proposal in effect says that markets can only charge de minimis fees. I find it shocking that anybody in business would want the prices that they charge capped at a diminimus level. What is your opinion on the access fee issue?

NICOLL: We think that it is a mistake. We think that it is a result of lobbying by price matchers. The people who are in the price matching business want to be able to lay off into agency markets at minimal cost. We think that the SEC has listened to their arguments (I was almost going to say 'to their whining' but I stopped myself) about agency fees for a long time. The fact of the matter is that we are (and ECNs in general are) a pure agency marketplace. I think I heard somebody before talk about the fact that ECNs do not provide capital, that they do not interact. This is absolutely correct. We never do and we never will because our customers do not want us to.

What we do is allow people who commit capital to the market to have the same fair access to the quotes as everybody else. We do not give one participant preference over another participant. We are a neutral agency broker, we are a neutral marketplace. We stand between buyers and sellers and we treat everybody the same. We collect a tiny, tiny fee to do that. That fee has gone down by over 90 percent in the last three years. Instinet, in the bad old days, used to capture five dollars for every thousand shares it traded. Today, Instinet captures less than 45 cents. That is what competition does.

Why the SEC finds it necessary to step in now is beyond me. I just do not understand it. It is wrong-headed, it is bad. I thought that we found out a long, long time ago that this command and control regulation is a mistake.

BRETT REDFEARN (Bear, Stearns & Co., Inc)[9] [From the Floor]: The Island ECN demonstrated that it was both willing and able, for over a year, to ignore the trade-through rule in the ETF products. Island actually got a significant amount of market share in the Qs. I would argue in part that that had to do with the nature of price discovery in the ETF products. Island was able to ignore the trade-through rule and the SEC did not enforce it for well over a year. Why wasn't the Island ECN able to attract any liquidity in listed products with the different price discovery process over that period of time?

NICOLL: If you do not think that the electronic markets will capture much of the floor based volume if the trade-through is abolished, then the only way we will find out is by allowing competition to play out. Again, the liquidity that the NYSE has is a powerful asset. If you floor based guys lose that liquidity to anybody, look in the mirror. You will only have yourselves to blame. You guys should be trouncing everybody. It is no surprise to me that it is difficult to compete with that block of liquidity that you provide. We are just asking for an opportunity to do so. Thank you very much.

SCHWARTZ: That was great. Thanks very much to you, Ed.

---

[9] At the time of the conference, Brett Redfearn was Senior Vice President at the American Stock Exchange. He is currently Senior Managing Director at Bear, Stearns & Co., Inc.

CHAPTER 3: OPERATIONS OF A FLOOR BROKER

Moderator – Robert Schwartz, Zicklin School of Business, Baruch College
Marvin M. Speiser
Professor of Finance and University Distinguished Professor
Paul Davis, TIAA-CREF Investment Management
Senior Managing Director
Robert Fagenson, Fagenson & Company
President
Robert McCooey, The Griswold Company
President & Chief Executive Officer
Doreen Mogavero, Mogavero, Lee & Company
President & Chief Executive Officer
Jamie Selway, White Cap Trading
Managing Director
Robert Shapiro, Iridian Asset Management
Director of Trading

ROBERT SCHWARTZ: The title of this session, 'Operations of a Floor Broker,' is fine for the program, but I would also like to focus on the value of a trading floor in our discussions. In numerous ways, the first panel and Ed Nicoll's speech set the tone today. With that, I would like to start by making sure that everybody knows the cast of characters on the panel. So, Bobby McCooey and Doreen Mogavero, will you confirm that you indeed are direct access brokers?

ROBERT McCOOEY: We are indeed direct access brokers.

DOREEN MOGAVERO: I am a direct access broker on the New York Stock Exchange.

SCHWARTZ: Thank you. We have two direct access brokers here. Next, look at who I have put in the middle – my two buy-side panelists, Paul

Davis and Rob Shapiro. On the far right is our specialist, Bob Fagenson. Why did I put Bob over there? He likes a post behind him so that he can look out over the crowd in front of him. Lastly, between the buy-side and the specialist, we have Jamie Selway. Jamie always says he represents the buy-side. Would you say a word, Jamie, so that people will know how you fit in here?

JAMIE SELWAY: We are an upstairs agency brokerage. We consume the floor services and some special services, and we use INET and Arca and other electronic systems as well. We are agnostics who view all these venues as competing providers.

SCHWARTZ: I would like to see the bigger picture. In so many of these debates, I constantly hear criticism. I hear, oh, this goes on, which is good, or that goes on, which is not good. Maybe I am shooting too high, but lets try to get the bigger picture. Let us first get a view of some of the benefits of what you the floor brokers do. I will turn to Bob McCooey's and Doreen's end of the table and ask what you two see as your service, your value added. Please tell us what you bring to the markets.

MOGAVERO: Very little is ever said about the catalyst effect of the information flow we provide to the trading experience overall. It has been my professional experience in over 25 years that many traders want to trade and want to buy stocks, but that they are very unsure of market conditions until I give them a clear market picture.

SCHWARTZ: You have what kind of a function?

MOGAVERO: Catalyst.

SCHWARTZ: A catalyst function. I find that very interesting. You get trading going. My co-authors, Archishman Chakraborty and Mike Pagano, refer to the difficulty of 'getting trading started' as 'a book building problem.' Another word that we use is 'animator.'

MOGAVERO: I do not like that word but it is one of the most important functions I provide to my clients. Knowing who else is in the market and what the current market looks like, gives my clients confidence that they can do exactly what they want to do.

ROBERT SHAPIRO: As a practitioner of the auction market system, I agree that, within the context of today's framework, when you need to do something of significant size, or of significant complexity, the best course of action is to go through the Doreen's and Bob McCooey's of the world. I do not think that is a point that necessarily needs to be debated.

SCHWARTZ: What do they do for you?

SHAPIRO: They can get within the fiber of the market dynamic around the specialist post and help you conduct a better trade. The problem is that that is principally the only game in town. If you believe that that's the case, they should, in effect, have better statistics versus an anonymous DOT order sent down to the floor. Your data, Bob, have captured that dynamic. I am not validating your study but, intuitively, I get the point. If you are working an order in the crowd and you have the ability to step in, to step out, to move things around, and to interact with the specialist, you can trade in a manner that an anonymous DOT order can't do. I want to make it clear that these people do have value today in the auction market.

MOGAVERO: Thank you.

SHAPIRO: Let me say a bit more about my background in addition to being a buy-side trader. My firm manages $10 billion. We are mid-cap and large-cap value players, and 95 percent of my trading flow is in listed stocks. Many times these stocks are not easy to trade. (I'll have something to say about that in a moment). In many cases, because of the captive liquidity that the New York Stock Exchange has, we are mandated, forced or obligated to enter that market center. I want to put this comment in context. When we choose the NYSE as the place to affect a trade, often it is the Doreen's and Bobby's of the world who provide a very valuable service. This is not necessarily an endorsement of the direct access model versus the upstairs model (I will get to that later). I am only talking about the brokers in the crowd in today's market environment. They provide a service that is very often valuable.

SCHWARTZ: What's your experience, Paul Davis?

PAUL DAVIS: I agree.

WOLF: I heard a wonderful presentation earlier by the CEO of Instinet, but I did not hear one word of concern about the needs of the institutional investor. I would like Paul Davis to explain why he is sending orders from his firm, TIAA-CREF, to the floor. Clearly, there is some added value to the floor. Maybe he can highlight where it comes from.

DAVIS: When you are talking about priorities, when you are talking about the NYSE, you have to take place into account. To simplify the equation, it is all place, price and time. Those are the rules. If you are going to trade in NYSE stocks, you play by the rules. You need intermediation and you need to be represented in the crowd. If I were to try to trade a large order electronically in an NYSE stock, I would probably get bagged because some person in the crowd could take advantage of my order.

So I play by the rules. But I am agnostic – if the rules change, I will play the game differently.

SHAPIRO: I should add that my decision to initiate a transaction on the floor of the New York Stock Exchange could come after I have exhausted other strategic alternatives. I could have tried desperately to find a match in Liquidnet and failed. I could have desperately tried to find liquidity in Arca and failed. I could have tried but failed to find liquidity in a crossing network like POSIT. Then, because the mandate of my firm is to grow and to protect assets, I must effectuate the investment directive of my portfolio manager. However, within the context of best execution, often the last choice is the New York Stock Exchange because it still aggregates a tremendous amount of liquidity.

We can all get on our soap boxes and say, 'I'm not going to trade there because I hate this and I hate that, but part of the NYSE's strategic big picture is to capture as much liquidity as it can and retain it. That will always make people like myself, so long as there are no alternatives to the New York, send my orders down to the exchange. In this case, often the best course is to utilize the Doreens and Bobbys.

SCHWARTZ: I have a question for Bob Fagenson. How do you capture liquidity, Bob?

ROBERT FAGENSON: Why do people send us orders? We like to think that we get business because we are providing a function that our customers feel is valuable. That function is obtaining the best price available by bringing the buyers and sellers together in a way that gives them the ability to obtain information and to make informed decisions based on good judgment.

People have said it is important to innovate, that it is important to offer different products. That's true. And that is why the New York Stock Exchange is going to offer an auto-execution capability at the inside quote.[10]

---

[10] In August 2004, after this conference was held, the NYSE announced the first version of its proposed hybrid trading platform. The plan came as the Securities and Exchange Commission stepped up pressure for market structure reforms in its proposed Regulation NMS plan. This comprehensive document recommended liberalizing the trade-through rule and also offered proposals on access fees, market data and subpenny trading. The NYSE said it would expand the NYSE Direct+ automated trading system, lift restrictions on the size and timing of orders and permit the cancellation of orders that are not immediately executed. The plan would also allow investors to buy and sell more shares in a system styled on ECN 'sweep' functions. By year-end, under pressure from various groups, including mutual funds, brokerage firms, ECNs and electronic players, the

It will be for those people who choose a nanosecond execution and to access that liquidity without being interfered with, without anyone else having a second guess. People who want this are entitled to it, and we will deliver it. But 85 to 90 percent of the time, the specialist's function is to bring buyers and sellers together with no friction, with no one in between, and to help the brokers and the agents, or the customers themselves, to get such pure information. It is naïve to expect all players to display their entire order size on either side. Historically, it's been a case of, 'you show me yours and I'll show you mine.'

People will always want to reserve their decision-making. They feel that if they give everything out all at once, they could be damaged. This is just what Paul said – the function of the NYSE is to aggregate liquidity. This has value, and that is why people use the exchange. If they did not think it was valuable, they wouldn't. We believe we have a dominant market share because we offer the best price and the best quality service. But it would not give the full picture to say that the exchange is a monopoly when 20 to 25 percent of our order flow is going elsewhere. And order flow does go elsewhere because other people are offering a business model that is attractive to them.

To be perfectly frank, when you choose with your feet and you send your order somewhere else, it is theoretically because you are getting something better. It is shame on us if we are losing that order flow. We are

---

proposal was revised. However, the new proposal still attracted controversy. Many critics, including the influential *Wall Street Journal*, said it was flawed. For instance, some institutional investors said the plan, as envisaged as of late 2004, unfairly allowed NYSE brokers to maintain a separate agency interest file of unpublished orders. This arrangement would allow brokers to work orders privately and electronically at auction. The NYSE proposed that at the best bid and offer, the broker was required to display 1,000 shares. The NYSE, moreover, said it was committed to fair access to the best prices on stock executions for investors across all markets, including the Big Board. Nevertheless, the Securities and Exchange Commission turned around in December 2004 and revised its Reg NMS plan. In particular, in one proposal the SEC recommended a voluntary system allowing access to the full depth of the NYSE book. NYSE CEO John Thain charged that the new Reg NMS plan could lead to the introduction of a CLOB, or central limit order book, which would, 'on a practical level eliminate the opportunity for a negotiated trade within the system.' The NYSE regarded the revised Reg NMS proposals as a severe blow to its plan for a hybrid market. In the end, if reforms are finally enacted, some analysts believe this would put the future of NYSE floor traders in doubt. These analysts were predicting the elimination of jobs on the floor as a result of increasing automation and more direct access.

competing. However, the fact that our competitors have not been gaining market share the way they did on NASDAQ – and have been complaining about anti-competitive rules – is because the NYSE has a far better form of liquid market. That's why our customers have stayed. It's something our competitors refuse to accept. They continue to whine and cry in an attempt to get Congress or the Securities and Exchange Commission to legislate into law their business model that just won't work.[11]

The ECNs succeeded tremendously in NASDAQ because they were right for that market. The market makers were lazy. Their markets were wide and, just as the International Securities Exchange (ISE) is succeeding in the options market because it's giving people a model they want, the ECNs are similarly attractive in the NASDAQ market. The ISE, in fact, has had to operate with in the context of a trade-through rule and yet it has achieved significant market share. Bernard L. Madoff Investment Securities, the largest independent market maker in listed securities, is another example of an entity that did not find it necessary to have rules changes to validate its business model. They have offered a service that investors want. Others have not succeeded in our market for the reason that roughly 95 percent of the time you find the best price at the place that offers the greatest liquidity – at the NYSE. Why go anywhere else?

SCHWARTZ: It is my impression that we tend to focus too much on the blue chips. My finding with Puneet Handa and Ashish Tiwari is that the value of intermediation services is greater for the smaller caps. It is also important to know when these services are not as necessary and can be done electronically. It is when they are not needed that you see the orders flowing to other markets.

SHAPIRO: Bob Fagenson finished his commentary by asking, 'Why go anywhere else?' The last time I spoke I said that I start with Liquidnet. Frankly, there are a number of trading venues for difficult to trade stocks where, if given the chance, I can find accessible liquidity with de minimus, if not zero market impact. I almost always choose that route prior to opening my trading dynamic to the floor mechanism. I talk about my

---

[11] Critics of the NYSE have lobbied for the reform and repeal of the trade-through rule. The rule is supposed to provide price protection at the best markets for customer orders. In reality, according to critics, customers sometimes obtain an inferior execution when, for instance, the order is not immediately executed on the NYSE at the best price. Indeed, in one set of revisions, the SEC proposed eliminating the trade-through rule for 'slow markets.' In another, the SEC proposed eliminating a provision which would have permitted investors to 'opt-out' of seeking the best price in favor of speedy executions.

praise and respect for Bobby McCooey's and Doreen's practice, and what Bob Fagenson's firm does going to the floor.

Going to the floor is sometimes my last resort for strategic reasons. I want to make that clear. It is not that I hate this or hate that. My job is to effectuate a trade as best as I can. Very often, given a lot of the negative consequences of being on the floor, I choose an alternative that is not floor based.

MCCOOEY: Rob, I think that is what we are talking about at the New York Stock Exchange. It is not just about competition, which our previous speaker talked about a lot. We are willing to compete and we are going to compete. As Bob Fagenson indicated, some 93 percent of the best bids and offers are at the NYSE, and this translates into 80 percent of the volume. At the same time, it is about customer choice. You choose the way that you are trading. You choose to use those alternatives first and then go to the floor. There are obviously others who choose a different dynamic. Some may choose to be in a system while they are checking out what is happening on the floor, through somebody who may be bidding part of his or her order in an ECN at the same time.

That is what we are continually striving for at the NYSE. It means giving more choices to customers, more electronic choices, and allowing customers to understand the choices that they have for accessing a floor broker – either a floor broker who uses direct access business models like Doreen and I, or a floor broker who uses an upstairs business model. It means allowing them to understand how they are talking with their floor brokers, and how the floor brokers are best servicing clients trying to bring the order flow to the stock exchange. We want to compete by offering choice.

DAVIS: It would be interesting to comment on Professor Schwartz's reference to price discovery.

SCHWARTZ: And quantity discovery.

DAVIS: Quantity discovery is very important. Large institutions need to find size. We want to find size first. That is why we go out to a Liquidnet or a POSIT. We are looking for size. Sure, we will slice and dice if there is no alternative, but slicing and dicing is not mission number one for me.

MCCOOEY: Paul, with all due respect, one of the services I provide in my information function on the floor is sending my customers in a direction where they can find that size. We can do that by understanding who have been the names in the stock. I can do this without knowing whether my customer is a buyer or a seller. I can send them in the direction of a large firm that may be the contra-side to their trade. And that does not put any commission in my pocket at the end of the day. They are going to trade with that natural buyer or seller with very little market impact, and to be able to do that in size.

I believe that Rob Shapiro has experienced this, and that others have experienced this when they come down to the floor. They can find that valuable information. One of the things we worry about when we push towards more and more automation, to become more of an electronic exchange, is that we will lose some of that crowd dynamic. If we do, we can lose some of that information flow that a lot of customers find valuable.

SCHWARTZ: The way I see it, quantity discovery is very much the issue that we were talking about with regard to book building. It is the issue that Avner Wolf and I have been looking at with Asani Sarkar in our study of the extent to which markets really are two-sided. We all accept that if there is a trade, there is a buyer and a seller, so the market must be two-sided. But the issue is far deeper than that. There are fundamental buying desires out there co-existing with fundamental selling desires, and the buyers and the sellers are often not meeting each other.

I would like to draw Jamie into the discussion.

MOGAVERO: There is a question out there.

BROOKE ALLEN (Maple Securities) [From the Floor]: Markets are liquid when natural participants do better by adding liquidity rather than by taking it. Yet most of the metrics that I see these days are all about markets being better because the market order gets filled faster, better, cheaper or whatever. It has been my experience (I have been trading for about 16 years) that when the spreads were wide – and I think there are academic studies that support this – you did better on average by providing liquidity and being patient.

One metric that seems to be lost is volatility. We may have markets in NASDAQ stocks, in Microsoft, for instance, that have bigger, deeper quotes and that trade more shares, but that seem to be much more volatile. All things being equal, I prefer less volatility to more volatility. And, of course, I prefer more liquidity to less liquidity. What are the metrics for the participant in the market who builds the book, who provides the liquidity?

Aren't they the ones who we should be caring about, not the guy who comes in with the market order and wants it filled within 20 milliseconds?[12]

FAGENSON: Absolutely right. There is no question that a lot of the things that we are doing in terms of the new automation systems are designed basically to incent the liquidity provider, to reduce some of the fear factor. We understand and we appreciate that going for that liquidity before you come to the floor is something we must compete against, and we are really going to try. A lot of the emphasis is just what the gentleman is offering, by incenting someone to feel more comfortable with putting sizeable liquidity on the book. They are not only going to get protected, but displayed in an accessible fashion so that other people will find that the quotes are firm, that the liquidity is firm, that the liquidity can be accessed without interruption or interference. That is a big key to market evolution. We are working very hard on it.

SELWAY: It sounds a lot like an ECN.

SCHWARTZ: Jamie, in your opinion, have we focused the problem a bit better? I think that you stated it well. The big problem is that the latent liquidity is there, how do you get it out in the open? How do you approach it, Jamie?

SELWAY: We use the floor as a last resort. We try to create liquidity upstairs using limit order books if we can. We try to attract a seller

---

[12] Mr. Allen provides the following amplification: When the minimum price increment was wide (12.5 cents, or even 6.25 cents) the cost to a natural market participant of crossing the spread was correspondingly large. Additionally, with few price points available, there was value in stating intentions early so as to get position in the order book. Under most circumstances (when the spread was high relative to expected volatility over the expected life the order), these incentives lead both parasitic and natural participants to behave in ways that made markets more liquid and transparent. The dominant (most profitable) parasitic strategies in those days had been ones that added liquidity while creating a stabilizing negative feedback to the system. Today, the desire to trade is likely to be expressed as a set of input parameters to an algorithm; and the participant with a large order is foolhardy to do otherwise. The interests of all participants no longer meet in any one place so as to clear at a price. Instead, systems interact, each trying to game the other. As they battle it out, they create a very large number of publicly visible small orders and executions designed to confuse the observer as to intended behavior. This effort to mislead generally fails, and today's parasitic participant does well to automatically analyze this huge evidence trail so as to glean the intention of others and then try to get in front of those intentions. Although such parasites might be profitable, their activities create a positive feedback on the system, thereby destabilizing it.

through an aggressively priced published quote. The last resort is to go to the floor. The systems do exist to bring buyers and sellers together.

MOGAVERO: If I may add something, you have to take into consideration the types of accounts that are represented. Not all accounts feel that the floor is the last place to go to. For many accounts, the floor is the place to go to because they need the information that we provide.

SHAPIRO: That is an excellent point. It pertains to the strategy and sophistication of the institutional trader. Much of what we are talking about today is the old model versus the new model. The old model was to outsource the shepherding of your order process to a floor operator. Today, there is a growing breed of buy-side trader who feels that the control of their orders should remain on their desktops. As arrogant as it may seem, many feel that they can do a better job working their orders than anyone on the floor, and they want control over it. But when you have control over the order dynamic, you need choice. To Bob Fagenson's credit, he points out that the NYSE is leaning towards creating a menu of alternative choices. I applaud that. I have yet to see definitively what the choices are or will be. But, when they come out and they are there, we will discuss them. At the moment, there is a very limited choice from the NYSE, and that causes a lot of the frustration.

I want to get back to something that Bob McCooey said. The essence of his statement was that price discovery occurs at the specialist's post. Further, it is the good work of the Doreens and Bob McCooeys of the world that help a guy like me find the sort of price point that we are looking for. I have heard statements from the largest institutions, including some of the most militant names out there on the buy-side, that we do not need the specialist posts. I have heard that I am price discovery, that I am the market. I have heard that if I am going to be 50 percent of the volume in a particular name, I do not need anything other than to know I am price discovery.

SCHWARTZ: Do you believe it?

SHAPIRO: I am going back to economics 101. I will tell you that, if I am the buyer, the seller will find me within the fabric of the market context.

SELWAY: That is certainly how I experienced it. When you are given an order to execute, you know when your order is 20 percent of average daily volume. At that point, the buy-side trader is price discovery – he or she is empowered. And, if you can do things electronically and provide liquidity (which means saving the spread and preserving information), those are good things for you to do.

FAGENSON: As long as you can get to the source of liquidity.

SHAPIRO: If you are in the wrong marketplace, then you are not going...

SELWAY: And that becomes – do not get me wrong, I mean liquidity provision is a difficult problem. Which ECN to choose? Should I go in via the DOT system? The devil is in those details.

MOGAVERO: You have to hope that the stock that you are looking to buy or to sell lends itself to that type of trading. I hate to bring it up, but consider an ImClone type of stock that is obviously illiquid. I do not know it. It does not trade on the New York. But it is a good example of what happens in a stock that is purely electronic when Bob Fagenson is not there to stop a sudden price jump from happening. There are lots of different dynamics that nobody talks about. Sure, it's ok if you are going to be in Microsoft and be 50 percent of the volume, but if you are in one of Bob Fagenson's illiquid stocks, you will have a serious problem if Bob is not there.

FAGENSON: Jamie's point was that what I was describing in terms of our electronic evolution sounds a lot like an ECN. In many ways it is. We have the largest ECN. We trade 110 million shares a day on NYSE's Direct+. But we have accountability and responsibility, two things that an ECN does not offer. That is why you can have an ImClone or some other situation where the customers are thrown under a bus. And the competing market centers, rather than unifying and trying to right the situation, let competitive forces take over to say, 'Who has the best system' and start trading unevenly. Customers find that their fills are suddenly canceled, that their profits are turned into losses, and no one takes the ultimate responsibility for customer protection.

SELWAY: Brokers do.

FAGENSON: Some may have, but some may not have. I know customers who have ended up out on a limb and out a lot of money because a market center made a decision unilaterally without giving everyone a chance to have some input into it. There is some danger there.

SCHWARTZ: I am surprised at what you said about price discovery and about buy-side traders feeling that they are responsible for it. It does not mesh with what I have heard, and it does not mesh with what I would think would be the case. I thought that buy-side traders are really concerned about their orders affecting prices. They very much want to pull back from an active role in price discovery. The work I am doing with Mike Pagano and Archishman Chakraborty shows that, if you come in too soon with an order, you affect the price adversely, that you get a better price if you hold off. That is one reason why the buy-side does not want to participate actively in price discovery.

If a stock trades at 50, people start thinking, oh, it is worth 50, as if 50 is some sort of inherent value. But work that I am doing with Avner Wolf and Jacob Paroush regarding price discovery considers an environment where some people think the stock is worth 55 and others think it is worth 45. In our environment, the stock trades between the two values and, if I handle my order differently as a buyer, the stock might not be trading at 50 but closer to 55. In other words, how a buy-side trader handles his or her order can affect the level that a stock trades at.

SELWAY: Price discovery might not be the right term. The issue here is customer facilitation and choice. Does the customer want to outsource his trade – for example, anonymously using electronic trading systems and DOT – or does the customer want to send the order to the floor where information could be leaked. Some customers have preference for one over the other – trading upstairs or on else the floor. Doreen pointed out that information sharing can benefit some clients, but for every client it benefits, it has to hurt someone else.

SCHWARTZ: As a panelist at one of Bill Freund's conferences a number of years ago, I got into a discussion with a buy-side trader who was sitting in the audience. He said that he participated in price discovery. I pursued the thought a little bit. 'You really like to participate?' I said. 'My orders affect it,' he responded. At this point I said, 'Would you want to be the person responsible for saying what the price should be?' 'Oh, my God, no,' he replied, almost falling off his seat.

The point is, nobody wants to take personal responsibility for price discovery, and I do not think that anybody should. Price discovery is a key economic function that, first and foremost, must be played by a system.

SHAPIRO: I respectfully disagree. I think there is a breed of buy-side trader who does assume responsibility for price discovery. When I am given an order, I do not go over various sorts of mental algorithms to achieve that order's objective. I am empowered with the obligation of making sure that the order is effectuated within the context of my best execution responsibilities. I get an order and two seconds later Liquidnet pings me – this is not an advertisement for Liquidnet – and I can trade that stock right then and there at 36 bucks or whatever. Right then and there, I have made a decision that that is the right price for me to move this amount of stock. My experience, TCA analysis, and ultimately the SEC's client reviews will determine whether or not that price discovery moment was a valid one.

But that is my responsibility. I have to effectuate this trade, and finding the equilibrium point where I can meet my contra is wholly my responsibility. And that gets back to choice. When you are pinged, you have to determine whether it is a good price for you. Someone else getting pinged might say, well, there could be some large Boston mutual fund company on the other side and I do not want to get picked off. You have to make that determination, and that is where you add value. We add value by understanding what is happening on the floor. Jamie Selway adds value by what he hears upstairs. Bob Fagenson adds value if he provides liquidity. There is a lot of value added and, as a buy-side trader, you must determine where that value is for any particular trade.

SELWAY: It probably makes sense that if the investment decision is based on who the other side is, you should take the ticket to the floor because then you can find that out. If it is not, if the portfolio manager just says I want to own it at 30, and if you have downward momentum to complete the ticket at 30 or below, go for it. ECNs are pretty well suited for that. ECNs provide anonymity whereas in a floor trade, the client may share information to get more information. Frankly, we are sort of self-selected. Our clients are the kind of folks who say, look, this is my bogey – if you can buy it below this bogey, buy the entire company. That is how we are disciplined by clients who provide prices.

SHAPIRO: Let's get back to Brooke Allen's argument about limit orders. Bob McCooey talked about incentivizing limit orders. That is good for the top 50 or 100 names that trade on the New York Stock Exchange and NASDAQ. But I do not think that there are too many in this room who will disagree that, in a secondary or a tertiary name, if you posted a 50,000 share bid or offer, the stock will simply move away from you. So, how do we incentivize limit orders in that kind of an environment? As soon as you post some kind of large liquidity, that stock is going to move away and that is going to disadvantage you.

SCHWARTZ: I would like to hear what Bob Wood has to say.

ROBERT WOOD (University of Memphis) [From the Floor]: I am going to change the topic a little bit. There is a groundswell of algorithmic trading. The algorithmic traders want instant execution. They want the ability to cancel instantly. The last time I was aware of it, specialists had 15 seconds before they had to cancel an order when the cancellation was submitted. Is that still the case, Bob?

FAGENSON: Order entry and cancellation are instantaneous. I think you are referring to ITS executions that have a 30-second turnaround to trade or to cancel. But, no, your order – as soon as you can get it into our system and it comes through the gateway...

WOOD: Over DOT?

FAGENSON: Yes. It will...

WOOD: It is done instantly?

FAGENSON: It does a check to see if there has been an execution before confirming a cancellation. It does an instantaneous check. But there is no delay

WOOD: Without specialist intervention?

FAGENSON: No, absolutely not. No specialist intervention.

WOOD: Unless it is over ITS?

FAGENSON: Yes, if you are sending the order from another market center, you cannot cancel it at once. It may not get auto canceled or executed for 30 seconds. A year from now, when we talk about this again, it will all be ancient history. Connectivity and smart routing will be the wave of the future. ITS in its present form will be anachronistic (if it is not already). It is just what we happen to have at the moment.

There is one other thing that we should focus on – the floor is at its best under stress. When a stock is trading benignly at the same price back and forth, it does not need an intermediary. We could create a floor based Liquidnet or anything else where institutions can find one another without anyone getting in the middle (if that truly were the Nirvana). Then we would not need me, we would not need any other intermediaries, and the sell-side could simply disappear.

But that just does not happen. It has not happened, and I do not see it happening any time in the future. When four sellers appear in a stock and you get that sudden volatility that you do not like, what happens on the floor of the exchange is that the person with accountability tries to find the other side. In the old days, you would have had thousands of trading halts in this type of volume and volatility environment while looking for the other side. Now the specialists are trying to work efficiently and effectively. They are trying to find the other side and keep the stocks trading.

The system happens to work very well. You take a look at the NYSE's specialist system, and at the ability of agents to bring the other side in effectively and efficiently using the electronics that are now in their hands. Forget pads and papers, those are things of the past. We shine in carrying out that price discovery function, particularly in the less liquid stocks. That is where you want the value added by someone who steps up to the plate. The system works magnificently well. If you have not seen it, you ought to come down and visit us and take a look at it firsthand. It is worth seeing.

DAVIS: I think it is time to criticize the NYSE a bit. We seem to all be saying how wonderful it is.

SHAPIRO: We thought Paul would be the one to do that.

DAVIS: They are schizophrenic here. The NYSE is trying to spend enormous amounts of money, and is trying to get into the direct trading business. The exchange is trying to become electronic on the one hand, and I think they will do so at the cost of the floor. I would like to see the shift more towards enhancing what happens on the floor, within the crowd, to get size meeting size. Size is not going to meet size with all the slicing and dicing that is going on. If the NYSE continues in the direction it is going in, it could simply become another ECN. Perhaps they are only paying lip service in not wanting to be another ECN. But, frankly, if you look at the floor of the exchange, too often you do not see much in the way of a crowd around a booth. The question is, is the crowd going away, and is the NYSE just going to become another ECN? I'll leave that as an open question.

SCHWARTZ: I would like to build on a word that Bob Wood mentioned. I think it relates to your point, Paul. The word that Bob Wood mentioned is algorithmic trading. I would like to put it in the context of so many discussions about what happens at the NYSE. We talk about what kinds of orders there are on the exchange. We commonly refer to market orders and limit orders. It is as though the exchange is primarily a limit order platform. It is not. The ECNs started as limit order platforms – and then they got fancier about it –, and there are electronic limit order platforms throughout Europe.

But the NYSE differs, in my opinion, in a very clear way. It is the exchange's floor brokers, the direct access brokers like Doreen and Bob McCooey bringing in the orders, and like Bob Fagenson, the liquidity-supplying lion keeper who keeps everybody in line as he integrates the orders. But the orders that are being worked on the floor are not called market orders or limit orders. They are not-held (NH) orders. The NH orders are terribly important, right? They agree, the NYSE panelists are all nodding their heads in the affirmative.

What is an NH order? It is very close to an algorithmic order. And what are you guys? You are human algorithms. As I see it, the question boils down to this. Why can't we do electronically what you human algorithms do on the floor? Now, Liquidnet is an attempt to do that.

MCCOOEY: What makes the NYSE different is that it makes either the specialist (if you choose to use him as your agent) or the floor broker (as your agent) accountable for understanding your order and meeting your needs and goals. At the end of the day, that agent is responsible for executing your order. That is what we do best as human beings. We think about the dynamics of trading and about what is going on in the marketplace. When the Federal Reserve makes a decision on rates, we make our trading decisions based upon what is going on at that moment in time. Our challenge is to remain relevant. We have done a good job so far and, with the use of better technology going forward, we will continue to be relevant.

MOGAVERO: Can I just say one thing about the division of control between upstairs and downstairs? I do not think of myself as controlling someone else's order. This is very much a team effort. Whatever information I can garner from the buy-side client about the order and about what his objectives are, and whatever information I can give him about what is going on in the marketplace, should meld as one. This is not about me controlling his order, or giving it to Bobby Fagenson to control. It is a matter of us working together.

SELWAY: That was not meant in an adversarial way.

MOGAVERO: No, no, no, I do not mean to take it as adversarial. But people do keep saying that it is either the folks upstairs, or us on the trading floor. It is not that way at all.

SELWAY: Because this is sort of an NYSE love fest...

MOGAVERO: As well it should be (laughter).

SELWAY: I would ask Bob McCooey what...

SCHWARTZ: The time to criticize has arrived, guys, turn them loose.

SELWAY: What does not work in Cisco then? We have talked about agents operating on the floor, we have talked about folks like me who are upstairs, and agents with clients' best interests at heart. What is missing in Cisco?

MCCOOEY: Cisco is a tremendous liquidity type of stock.

SELWAY: Cisco is naturally twice as liquid as IBM?

MCCOOEY: I do not know the stats on Cisco versus IBM in terms of market cap, in terms of shares outstanding, or in terms of average trading volume. I do not know that they are equal. I also think that IBM trades at about $95 a share and that Cisco trades at about $22...

SELWAY: If you compare the top ten most liquid NASDAQ names with the top ten NYSE names, I think that you would see, from a statistical standpoint, from the way financial economists think if it, market quality is bigger in the NASDAQ names. I am simply asking if that suggests that anything is missing.

FAGENSON: They may be missing market efficiency there. We take a look at NASDAQ stocks all the time, and we study how many shares have to trade to move a share from a real buyer to a real seller, to someone who ultimately wants to own the stock from someone who ultimately wants to dispose of it, or to someone who just wants to day trade it. One heavily traded NASDAQ stock took 38 shares of trading to move one share from one place to another.[13] The market may be highly liquid, but the system appears to be highly inefficient when you look at the goals that you are espousing for your customers.

We also have to consider the size and nature of the institutions that trade. Everyone is not as sophisticated as them. Everyone does not have the heft that the 800-pound gorilla –which we may pretend to ignore – can bring into a marketplace. You do not have that 20 percent participation in the stock from everyone. The Midwest bank that wants to buy or to sell 17,000 shares has an entirely different set of parameters within which it must operate.

The issue is, if we can achieve the satisfaction of customer goals collectively, either you will individually go first to whichever liquidity provider suits you best, and ultimately wherever you think you will have to go to get the job done if your first choice does not work. The one thing that we do not want to be (and which many people are) is captives of mediocrity. Take the volume weighted average price, for instance. With VWAP, people are being paid to be average. To the extent that this is the case, I suggest that we are all being over-paid, that we should all be doing something else. But our system is geared to deliver the better product. We work in tandem

---

[13] Critics of the NYSE have lobbied for the reform and repeal of the trade-through rule. The rule is supposed to provide price protection at the best markets for customer orders. In reality, according to critics, customers sometimes obtain an inferior execution when, for instance, the order is not immediately executed on the NYSE at the best price. Indeed, in one set of revisions, the SEC proposed eliminating the trade-through rule for 'slow markets.' In another, the SEC proposed eliminating a provision which would have permitted investors to 'opt-out' of seeking the best price in favor of speedy executions.

with whatever our customers want, whether we are first on the list or third on the list is less significant than if we are all working together to achieve their goals. This is not an issue of control.

MCCOOEY: Jamie, a follow-up observation regarding the SEC execution numbers that Ed Nicoll spoke about. The way that those numbers are calculated is very suspect. If there are 10,000 shares offered and a 50,000-share buy order comes in and it takes the liquidity on the 10,000 shares, and then the remaining 40,000 shares trade higher, that is price dis-improvement. But 50,000 were not offered, so there is no reason why that should be held as dis-improvement against the NYSE. We take issue with the way the SEC calculates those numbers.

Secondly, Ed also cited the NASD advertisement. We would think it would be much better to look at that in terms of basis points with regard to the stocks in the S&P 500 that are very low-priced stocks and their spreads are very narrow in those low-priced stocks. In terms of basis points, we can show you statistics that demonstrate that our market quality is much better than theirs.

SELWAY: Surveys show, time and time again, that institutional clients are more satisfied with the NASDAQ product than they are with the NYSE product. Are the surveys just wrong?

MCCOOEY: We have gone through some challenges over the past year Jamie, that may skew people's thoughts about the NYSE, even in regard to execution. We have gone through a problem with our former chairman, we have had some other issues that we have been challenged with over the past year, and I would certainly like to allow the changes that we have proposed to take hold for six months or so. Then let us take that survey again and see whether or not we score a lot better. I believe that we will score better.

DAVIS: Let me speak also to Jamie's question from a trading cost point view. Frankly, the NASDAQ model works also. Trading costs in NASDAQ are roughly the same as they are in the NYSE. No matter how I try to measure them, I get pretty much the same results. And I am getting the same results on international trading as well. It is a pretty good world right now for traders. Our trading costs have come down, and volatility seems to have come down. Maybe it is the competition that is in play right now, with everyone hustling after the order flow. But right now is a pretty good time.

FAGENSON: You are really on to something. We have found historically that every time markets have innovated, that every time we have brought the customer closer to the point of sale, business has exploded. We have become the beneficiaries of our own efficiencies, and that will continue. As Bobby said, if we watch the next six months as we go through our next evolution, the same thing will happen. This is not something to be feared. It is something to be welcomed and we do welcome it. We will all be the beneficiaries of this as it comes to pass.

SCHWARTZ: We have somebody waiting patiently in the back of the room.

DAVID DUSENBURY (Dionis Capital) [From the Floor]: My question is for the broader panel. From the buy-side perspective, what changes would you like to see at the NYSE? From the perspective of those of you who make your money off the floor, what changes do you think are going to happen?

DAVIS: I have been an advocate of something that I call a virtual crowd. What I advocate would expand the crowd to include liquidity, from buy-side institutions, and it can be done electronically. To give you a first step in that direction, if I want to trade a stock I would like to look in my Bloomberg and see how many people are in the crowd, including buy-side institutions. If I see that no one is in the crowd, I will start slicing and dicing in trading this stock.

SHAPIRO: I would like to see something that dovetails into something that Bobby was saying. There are reams of data that suggest that one market structure –a centralized model like the NYSE is better than the other, a decentralized model like NASDAQ But at the end of the day, let's just say they are equal. However, on the NYSE side of the coin, if they are only one-third as good as their statistics deem them to be, for the life of me, why do not they just open it up to competition? They are the best model. The specialists are the best at finding liquidity. Doreen and Bobby are the best at providing information and at helping me manage my trading dynamic. Open the gates of competition and level the playing field. If they really are one-third as good as they claim to be, I do not see what the problem is. I do not want a protectionist facility in place here. I want choice. I want to see the competition, to know how I can trade my stocks.

SCHWARTZ: I would like to ask you two guys, can you see pulling in electronic algorithmic trading and integrating it with the floor?

SHAPIRO: Absolutely. Right now we do algorithmic based trading, but it is 'algomanual.' So you have micro market makers spinning orders down onto the floor, and then you have some terribly gifted person literally creating the contra-side to those orders. If that person somehow gets (I am supposing) replaced by a black box that can counter the algorithmic logic, that becomes an algorithm based model. There is no reason why Bobby McCooey and Doreen cannot retrain one part of their skill set to interact with it, and potentially also live alongside the Bob Fagensons of the world and allow them to do their superlative job with all of the stuff that they do. I am not here to put a bullet in their head. However, if they say that they are the best, then why can't they compete with the best of the best?

DAVIS: Let me answer that too. We have a pause feature in our own algorithmic models so that, at any point in time, while the model is trading, we can put it on pause. If we had a virtual crowd and I suddenly saw a half a dozen people in the crowd, I would put it on pause. I would call Doreen or Bob McCooey and ask them to work the order. When they were done, if I still had stuff left, I would take it off the pause mode and let the algorithmic trading continue to go.

SCHWARTZ: I am curious. We got a very strong statement from the buy-side as to what would enable the three of you to operate more effectively. Do you like that statement? Is it something to build on?

FAGENSON: Intellectually we are not that far apart on this stuff. We all want to bring the customers what they want. That is the only way we thrive. But when you talk about not being able to compete, I am not sure that I follow. Look at Bernie Madoff. Madoff came in, competed magnificently, did not ask to change anything, and took ten percent of the volume. What makes you think that someone with a model that is attractive to you cannot compete? I do not understand that.

SHAPIRO: Liquidnet is on the verge of having its biggest volume day in the history of its existence today, as we speak. I suggest that it is very much under way. What I do not understand is whether or not the crux of what we are really talking and dancing around is the revocation of the trade-through rule. The rule, as you know, is a protectionist measure meant to keep market share on the floor of the NYSE. If you guys are as good as you claim to be, I just beg you to do away with that rule and prove your mettle. If you are the best there is, you will get 100 percent of my liquidity and you will put these other guys out of business.

But make no mistake. There is a movement underway by the buy-side community to direct volume to alternative trading systems that have liquidity and a style of trading that suits their needs. The movement may be a glacier-like, it may be a matter of behavior and old world notions. Maybe it will take another generation of traders who are trained on Gameboy to come in and change it. I do not know how it will happen, but it is happening. It is happening real time.

SCHWARTZ: Do you agree, Jamie?

DAVIS: The genie is out of the bottle.

SCHWARTZ: Do you agree, Jamie?

SELWAY: I do. To me, the trade-through rule is protectionist. New York has 80 percent of the liquidity. They should go out and prove their value. Remove the rule. Brokers are not going to trade-through; brokers will not ignore an electronically accessible price that is superior just to trade-through. That would be a great way to lose the next order.

FAGENSON: If people want to compete on price, there is the ability now to do so. We just do not believe we should remove the necessity for people to go to where the best price exists. The fact that we happen to have been here a long time and have the 80 percent market share is not strictly the result of protectionism and momentum/ We do not think throwing the flood gates open would be a positive step. A player in the airline industry would hopefully not start an airline that is very cheap but unsafe. History has proven in our industry that very often the participants who seek to make structural changes for their own advantage are not necessarily focused on what's best for the customer. Therefore, someone should be around to say that these models, in fact, are not necessarily great for the customer. Not everyone is as capable of protecting themselves as you guys are. What you might think is protection for us is the ultimate customer protection, which is to go to where the best price exists. If the issue that has been brought up by the competition so repeatedly is certainty, and we deliver certainty, then what is the problem with the trade-through rule?

SHAPIRO: There is absolutely nothing certain about an NYSE quote, trust me.

FAGENSON: What we are saying is that, if we remove the uncertainty by giving you autoex access to that quote, you would have the same ability as anyone else, unless they get there first. Then what is the issue?

SHAPIRO: It could happen...

FAGENSON: A year from now, call us on it.

SHAPIRO: I would love to reconvene.

SCHWARTZ: We have to move on. Thank you, everybody.

CHAPTER 4: ACHIEVING BEST EXECUTION THROUGH MARKET STRUCTURE DEVELOPMENT

Moderator–Theodore Aronson, Aronson+Johnson+Ortiz
Managing Principal
Arthur Hogan, Jefferies & Company, Inc.
Chief Market Analyst
William O'Brien, Brut, LLC
Chief Operating Officer
Richard Rosenblatt, Rosenblatt Securities Inc.
Chief Executive Officer
Lanny Schwartz, Philadelphia Stock Exchange
Executive Vice President & General Counsel
Michael Simon, International Securities Exchange
Senior Vice President & General Counsel
Wayne Wagner, Plexus Group
Co-Founder & Chairman

THEODORE ARONSON: Now it is time to bridge a gap. We are going to talk about market structure and some developments in the area of best execution. What do we know today about best execution that we did not know 10 or 20 years ago? We know that it is not a magic number. It is not a single number. Actually, it is a process. It is a process that depends on strategy and client objectives.

Here are the overarching questions for this panel: Do we have the tools and the appropriate market structure to effect best execution for all of our different needs? Who are the intermediaries who help us? Who are the intermediaries who hurt us? Who are the missing intermediaries and the intermediaries who should be absent from the picture?

As we all know, this is an extremely active period in our markets.

There are proposed changes from the Big Board, the NASD, the SEC and, heaven knows, soon maybe the Justice Department. So, with that, I turn to Wayne Wagner, who is a perfect bridge between this panel and the last panel. I would like him to share some statistics.

WAYNE WAGNER: I asked Ted to let me go first because I have some numbers that support what Paul Davis was saying in the last session. Paul was speaking largely about measurement, and partly from intuition. We at the Plexus Group have been looking at NASDAQ versus NYSE trading every quarter for God knows how long, but I got a big surprise when I looked at the numbers. I divided the stocks into five capitalization groups: giant-cap, large-cap, medium-cap, small-cap and micro-cap. The numbers include commission impact and our definition of delay or timing. That refers to how long it takes you to get to the point where you can actually affect a trade. Here are some cost numbers. Giant-cap is 30 basis points (bps) on the New York Stock Exchange and 43 basis points on NASDAQ. Large-cap is 56 bps on New York and 71 bps on NASDAQ. NYSE also scores betters on mid-cap: 81 bps vrs 85 bps for NASDAQ. It is only when you get to the small-caps and micro-caps, that you find a dramatic difference in numbers at the NYSE and NASDAQ. I think that is a function, not so much of the exchange mechanism, as of the nature of the product traded. This makes it very confusing because you wind up doing an apples and oranges kind of comparison.

At first, these numbers surprised me. Then I spent some time thinking about them. I realized that what I saw is exactly what you would expect in a situation where exchanges have been pitted against one another to deliver the best possible execution. As was noted in the last panel, these trading decisions are being made on the buy-side trading desks. The buy-side desks are under a best execution edict that Ted Aronson and the Association for Investment Management and Research – AIMR – put together. The desks choose the best execution. The net effect is that they are all converging towards the same idea. The technology is in place. We just have to learn to use it a bit better with linkages and algorithms.[14]

---

[14] The SEC's package of Reg NMS reforms in April 2005 respond to this idea from Wagner. In Rule 610, the regulator required, 'a uniform market access rule that would promote non-discriminatory access to quotations displayed by SRO trading centers through a private linkage approach.' The SEC also required SROs to use uniform trading rules. 'Rules that, among other things, prohibit its members from engaging in a pattern or

ARONSON: Thank you, Wayne. I appreciate that. Richard Rosenblatt, I have a question. What is the big deal about this trade-through rule and the changes that are recommended, and why the hell should we care?[15]

RICHARD ROSENBLATT: The trade-through rule has been in the spotlight much more than it was previously. I hope it enjoys the attention, because it is really not about trade-through. I currently spend some of my time upstairs on a trading desk, but I start every morning on the floor of the exchange with Bobby Fagenson and Doreen Mogavero. I trade-through orders all day long. I have always traded through. The rule does not prohibit it. The trade-through rule does not speak to that. The trade-through rule simply says that if you trade-through somebody who is offering stock at a better price, and if they ask you to fill their order, then you have to do so. My institutional clients do not really care about the thousand shares that were offered somewhere. They do not want to miss the 50,000 shares. So, I buy the 50,000 first. Normally the thousand shares disappear very quickly as soon as I have traded through them, but so be it. If the thousand shares would like me to buy their stock at the price that they are displayed at, I buy them. Why not? I think that we are talking about best price. I do not think that we are talking about the trade-through rule. Let's keep this simple.

I have heard a lot about the New York Stock Exchange today. I trade a lot there. I also trade a lot on the ECNs. The problem is sunshine. The problem is access. We are basically moving into an era of 'do-it-yourself' stock execution. My clients are getting smarter, they have more tools. My role as an agent is changing. I am becoming something of a consultant. The orders that I receive are evolving into something different. And it is all good stuff.

The trade-through rule makes all the sense in the world. If we are going

---

practice or displaying quotations that lock or cross the protected quotations of other trading centers,' according to the SEC.

[15] The SEC's package of Reg NMS reforms in April 2005 respond to this idea from Wagner. In Rule 610, the regulator required, 'a uniform market access rule that would promote non-discriminatory access to quotations displayed by SRO trading centers through a private linkage approach.' The SEC also required SROs to use uniform trading rules. 'Rules that, among other things, prohibit its members from engaging in a pattern or practice or displaying quotations that lock or cross the protected quotations of other trading centers,' according to the SEC.

to have accurate price discovery, then if I make an offer in an ECN or anywhere else at a better price, that should give me an advantage. You cannot argue the importance of limit orders and then say, 'but only my limit order counts, yours does not count.' The problem is access. As someone mentioned earlier, you want certainty of execution. If you see stock offered at $20 and you want to buy it, you do not really care if you get that stock in a millisecond. You want the certainty of knowing that $20 is the worst you are going to do in a millisecond. We currently do not have a marketplace trying to discover price where you can benefit, but where you cannot be hurt.

If the New York Stock Exchange wants to remain valuable, it has to solve this certainty of execution problem. The problem is not the trade-through rule. You want to know that if you send an order to the New York Stock Exchange, and the stock is offered at $20, that you bought it. End of story. But they do something down there that is pretty good. They discover price better than anybody else in the world. Every order creates a number of pricing opportunities that floor brokers, a specialist, or you, can take advantage of. The more options that you have, the more accurate the price will be.

To be radical, I will say that the New York Stock Exchange should not do autoex. Instead, it should do 'auto guarantee.' If you send in an order to buy those thousand shares at 20, you should instantly get a report saying that you bought a thousand shares at no worse than 20. Then let them try to do what they do well, which is to find the right price. If you buy the shares at 19.75, I do not think that you will complain. If that takes three, four, or five seconds, it is not going to hurt. Of course, you do not want to be tied up and have your bookkeeping in a mess, but five seconds is not going to hurt.

Sunshine is the best policy. Let's say the NYSE put this in an algorithm. You put in your thousand shares to buy at 20, you get your instant certainty of execution, and suddenly it becomes your 19.95 bid for five seconds. Somebody hits your bid and you did better. If instead somebody reacts by offering at 98 and you execute at that price after five seconds, you still did better. Why not? Let the New York Stock Exchange prove its value proposition. But do not push the exchange into a corner where it will automate its value out of existence. That does not make sense.

ARONSON: Bill O'Brien, how do you and your colleagues at Brut feel about that?

WILLIAM O'BRIEN: Dick Rosenblatt points out that it is not necessarily a price versus speed distinction, but rather a price versus certainty distinction. To the extent that the NYSE solves the problem that its quotes really are not accessible on an automated basis, then many of these issues will recede into the background. All investors would make a rational decision to execute against a quote on an automated basis that is a better price. The problem is that we are not there today. We have heard a lot of promises of things to come, but almost no detail. It remains to be seen whether there will be a meaningful solution to this problem over the short to intermediate term. Given that there is not a solution in the short to intermediate term, you have to allow traders to bypass liquidity that is not meaningfully accessible.

ARONSON: Let's continue with the left wing of this panel. Art Hogan, what is Jefferies' take on all of this?

ARTHUR HOGAN: This is all very interesting. One of the unintended consequences of decimalization is the recent release of Reg NMS by the SEC. All of the talk that we have heard today about the trade-through rule is encapsulated in that release, and we are currently in a 60-day comment period. Dick Rosenblatt has a terrific comment that you can read on the SEC's Website. I believe it is titled, 'Clearing Up the Myth of the Trade-Through Rule.'

ROSENBLATT: Close to that.[16]

HOGAN: The fact that we are here and talking about this is clearly an unintended consequence of what has happened to us because of decimalization. That being said, I would add that the argument of price discovery and certainty is posing a threat to the individual investor. I am not saying that an institutional investor does not represent individuals because it certainly does. The participants who are aggregated in retirement and pensions funds are certainly individual investors. However, that being said, your example of, 'I want to get the 50,000 shares at 20,' and 'I trade-through that person who is offering a thousand shares,' does not address the problem that the person who is offering a thousand shares at a better price is not going to get that trade-off. That is one thing that we have to be conscious of

---

[16] The proper title is, 'Debunking the Myths of the Trade-Through Rule: A View from an Agent.' The paper is referred to in a Comment Letter filed with the SEC by Rosenblatt Securities. A copy is posted on the firm's Website, www.rbit.com (See, market structure corner).

while we are waiting to see how the SEC comes down on this.

Have decimalization and the de minimus spreads that we see proved the trade-through rule to be archaic? Probably. Is there a better way to handle it than making it go away? Certainly. A better approach is to give the New York Stock Exchange a much more updated access to and from other market centers. If you were to look at the technology that the ITS system is running on now, as a stereo, it would be comparable to an eight-track. What we need is to get them a DVD player. We must make the other marketplaces accessible, including regional exchanges and ECNs.

I do not necessarily think we have to change the rule. I think we need to change the access to the New York Stock Exchange.

O'BRIEN: I agree totally. As a matter of fact, I would take it to the next step. I want Paul Davis to have that fast access to the markets also.

ROSENBLATT: The important point is that, if you have the access, the need for the trade-through rule falls away. What you would then have is a NASDAQ-like environment where no rule exists because there is no need for one. People act rationally.

ARONSON: Bill Harts, do you have a question?

WILLIAM HARTS [From the Floor]: It seems to me that it would be good to get some quantification around what all these changes might actually mean to the marketplace. You have people who say that the trade-through rule is customer protection. They say that it is very important to the market. Those people would obviously think that, if it were to go away, it would mean a deterioration of volume for the New York Stock Exchange. What I am trying to get my arms around is, by how much?

Brut is arguing for eliminating or weakening the trade-through rule for floor brokers like Dick Rosenblatt. How much volume would leave the New York Stock Exchange without the trade-through rule?

O'BRIEN: I will answer that from Brut's perspective. The fairest and most accurate answer, given my limited skills, is that I do not know. Unfortunately, we have couched the question in terms of either/or. Either the market should be fully electronic, or it should, by and large, be manual at the core. I think that there is room for an 'and' in there. Even in the electronic environment, no one system can meet the needs of all investors. Even if a trade-through rule were no longer to exist, it does not mean a fully electronic market will garner 80 percent, with a manual market relegated to a smaller percentage. But what there will be is fair competition without barriers to access, or to deploying your business model to your customers.

In the end, the market will judge what model is the most valuable and to what degree.

ARONSON: Bill, I did not hear a number in that response.

O'BRIEN: Will the New York Stock Exchange still have 80 percent market share? No. Will it be 48 percent? I would not be surprised. It also depends on your time horizon. People are slow to change.

ARONSON: I would guess 32 percent. Anybody else want to take a guess? Yes, Mike?

MICHAEL SIMON: As a representative of an options market, I am looking at this with interest, but it has no direct application to our market. People are assuming that Reg NMS is saying that the trade-through rule goes away. It does not. If you read Reg NMS carefully, it actually imposes, depending on your perspective, a worse trade-through rule than we have now. Right now, as Rosenblatt said, there is no penalty for trading through. You do not go to jail. What happens is that you have to protect somebody's order if you trade-through it and if they complain.

What they are proposing is what I call the 'criminalization' of trade-throughs. If you engage in a pattern or practice of trading through under Reg NMS, you have violated an exchange rule. That is what Lanny Schwartz and I face every day in the options market. The SEC has already forced us to do it. It forced the options exchanges to adopt an intermarket linkage that provides for disciplinary action if members trade-through. In the current equity world, a trade-through subjects you only to economic liability, not discipline. So, by subjecting a broker dealer to disciplinary action, the SEC made us criminalize trade-throughs. It is an unworkable rule. It is worse than a rule where you are simply providing protection for customer orders.

But I do not think that, even with an opt-out rule, the SEC's proposal will hurt the New York Stock Exchange if it goes into effect, especially with small orders. The opt out is only going to help the big institutions. It is not going to help the small investors. You are still going to have trade-through liability. The SEC made opting out so onerous – it must be case-by-case, not a blanket instruction – that it is not feasible for brokers to provide this to the small investor. Any broker who regularly sends orders to an ECN that does not provide trade-through protection simply is going to have to protect the orders they trade-through. ECNs will not be able to attract and retain order flow if they do not provide some assurance of best execution. Those brokers would be going, figuratively speaking, to jail if they violate the SEC's rule. It is a fundamentally flawed position and the SEC has not justified it at all.

O'BRIEN: That is why the current operation of the rule is so detrimental to electronic markets. We suffer the worst of both worlds. We do comply with the current rules on our automated basis, but the NYSE, quite frankly, does not. Brut is traded through by the New York Stock Exchange hundreds of times a day. I am sure that Archipelago can give you similar statistics. It puts us at a disadvantage because we cannot give customers who prefer an automated execution with certainty, regardless of the existence of superior prices on manual markets. At the same time, customers who are more driven by a duty of best execution to their own customers are hesitant to place limit orders on our system because the primary market ignores their prices. I struggle to understand how the New York Stock Exchange can advocate the existence of a trade-through rule from a customer protection standpoint when it wantonly disregards the rule.

HOGAN: The argument can be made, however, that primary markets are ignoring ECNs limit orders because there is an access fee and limited access, especially from the New York Stock Exchange to the ECNs in terms of connectivity.

O'BRIEN: I would disagree. Brut (and I) have talked about access fees a lot. I would not be surprised to see, in the future, more automated accessibility to the quotations. It is reflective of a theme that has been underlying a lot of the previous panels – limit orders have value. The willingness to provide liquidity has value, and fee structures have evolved over time to reflect this. As decimalization and other shocks to the more traditional liquidity provider community have forced them to deploy more agency-like models and to widen their spreads, other firms have leapt into the fray on a more automated basis to provide liquidity by taking that value into account. Many firms, the large majority of Americans, and probably the majority of the financial community that we have not heard from before, are providing liquidity to the marketplace based on a fee structure that reflects the fact that liquidity has value.

The bigger risk, especially to institutional traders, is that, to the extent that those access fees are regulated unnecessarily, costs go up. There are a large number of transaction-based costs that specialists have to bear – for instance, the New York Stock Exchange fees and SEC charges. But I do not think that is the overriding factor preventing specialists from going out. Especially given the fact that they have a mechanism to come to, like Brut and Archipelago, or ITS, that is free.

ARONSON: Lanny Schwartz from the Philadelphia Exchange.

LANNY SCHWARTZ: I would like to go back to a point that Mike Simon was making about the options markets. The options markets are extremely competitive, and the landscape has changed dramatically, in part because of the success of the ISE since its introduction in 2000. The trade-through rule has been an important factor in shaping that competitive landscape, but there have been other things as well – technology, rules, fees, quotes with size, the extension of the firm quote rule, payment for order flow, internalization and other things have changed the competitive landscape. So I would not assume that the trade-through rule alone would wildly affect the competitive landscape in the equities market. There are too many other variables.

SIMON: It is important to note that people are implying that you cannot compete against an entrenched floor-based manual market with a trade-through rule in place. Here's an example on the opposite side. On May 25, 2000, the ISE had zero percent market share. We started operations that were entirely electronic in a marketplace that had a trade-through rule. We have been relatively successful and we are now the largest equity options exchange. The key to our success has been two-fold. One, we provide the best prices. Two, we provide access to those prices. That is how an electronic market can compete against floor-based markets. I agree with Lanny Schwartz. We provided trade-through protection long before it was mandated by the SEC, and we continue to provide it today subject to criminal liability for our members if they do trade-through. On best execution, it is easy to create that model – provide the best price and give people access to that price.

L. SCHWARTZ: The trade-through rule and the linkage system have not biased the market either in favor of the ISE or in favor of the Philadelphia Stock Exchange. A more traditional floor-based exchange has increased its market share over time in that same environment.

ARONSON: There are hundreds in the audience, and nobody questions anything that has been said?

ROSENBLATT: Ted, can I take one final shot at this thing? First of all, I would answer Bill Harts' question. The answer is zero. The exchange has a huge challenge to automate. We heard it here. The exchange's problem is making its access more efficient so that all of you are happy with the speed and efficiency of reaching the markets anywhere, including the NYSE. What confuses me, and I think I can solve your problem, is that it is exactly the trade-through rule that protects you. You have an automated market. When you are traded through, simply program your system to instantly send a trade-through complaint to the offending exchange.

OBRIEN: There is the best execution obligation of our customer to his or her customer, and, to the extent that they miss the best possible price, these customers are not willing to take that risk because of the strong regulatory scrutiny of their best execution obligations.

ROSENBLATT: But that is my point. You are offering. Do not remove your offer. If somebody buys your stock after you made the complaint, you have got an execution. You have no obligation to the market center that traded through you. On the other hand, if the stock moves away from you and you were traded through, you will get a commitment from the offending exchange, New York or anywhere else, and your customer will be taken care of. So, it is the trade-through rule itself that, with a little programming, will protect you from disadvantaging any of your customers.

OBRIEN: I think that you have failed to comprehend how that entire dynamic strongly dis-incentivizes best execution driven customers from using an electronic system.

ROSENBLATT: Well, ignorance has always been one of my strong suits, so (laughter)…

OBRIEN: I am not accusing you of that. It is just a question of theory versus the reality.

ARONSON: I have a question over here.

THOMAS DOYLE (Nutmeg Securities) [From the Floor]: I want to reemphasize something that Paul Davis said in the last panel. He hit it right on the head. Ted, as you know, I kicked around the lower part of Manhattan for over 25 years. For the last eight, much like Dick Cheney, I have been operating from an undisclosed, remote location. Nevertheless, I have been electronically achieving pretty interesting results executing institutional sized orders. I have been seeing more consistent basis point results along the lines of some of the numbers that Wayne mentioned.

I have the following thought. As the gross commission top line gets squeezed, there is more of an incentive for brokers like us to go electronic. The cost of operating on the floor continues to increase while the cost of computerization continues to go down. At some point, that has to burst, break, or change. Right now, there is no incentive for people like myself to do anything but slice and dice orders. That is where the stock exchange, as Paul Davis said, has to make the effort. The exchange must bring us all out from being slicers and dicers.

ARONSON: A question from the front of the audience, please.

JAMES ANGEL (Georgetown University) [From the Floor]: Mike Simon made an interesting comment about the ISE's successes with a trade-through rule or practice in place. What is the difference between the options market and the equity market that enables the ISE to be a success, whereas the ECNs that have been trying for decades have not had the same level of success with NYSE stocks? I would like the gentlemen from both Brut and the ISE and everyone else to chime in on this.

SIMON: In the name of full disclosure, before I came to the ISE, I spent 11 years representing the New York Stock Exchange and ITS in market structure. I really do not see why the ECNs cannot compete today in the listed market. I do not think it is a good business model if ECNs continue to provide trade-throughs without a trade-through rule. I do not think that customers who come into the market from a best execution standpoint will accept a pattern of trade-throughs. Providing investors with executions that are inferior to what they could receive in other markets, is not a good business model. The ECNs will have to improve the quality of their quotations so that they are not traded through. That is the way we did it in the ISE. We provided the best price. Unless you provide the best price, trade-throughs are going to be a problem whether or not they are criminalized. They will be a problem whether or not you have to provide satisfaction, or whether or not it is simply the best execution obligation. I think that the ECNs can compete in today's environment.

O'BRIEN: I do not have options market experience commensurate with Mike Simon's, but I will offer two hypotheses. First, the nature of the order flow providers in the options space, and the regulatory scrutiny of execution quality in the options space (given that options order flow is not typically retail or mutual fund driven) changes the dynamic quite a bit. Traditional players are hesitant to explore alternative platforms.

Second, you cannot deny that, in the options market over the last three to five years, there has been significant regulatory intervention to break down barriers to competition. Today, we have multiple listing of options classes across various destinations. This was not the case five years ago.

Mandated linkage is really the regulators forcing change to open up competition and to give venues like the ISE equal opportunity. I believe that, to a lesser extent, we are asking for the same thing in the equities market.

SIMON: Eighty percent of our order flow is retail. We have very little institutional order flow. I think that we are under stronger scrutiny from the regulators in the area of best execution. The SEC, while mandating more competition, did so by specifically ordering us to have a trade-through rule and to have a linkage. Again, I think that it is doable.

ARONSON: Wayne, let me direct this to you. You have been especially thoughtful over the years on the subject of market makers versus ECNs or alternative strategies, most recently in the lead article in the Journal of Investment Management.[17] In the olden days it was obviously 100 percent human. Now some say that the trading process is somewhat subhuman. But do we need them both, and where are we headed?

WAGNER: In my opinion, the speakers have conceded that there is a division between the two. Things can flow electronically rather simply, with buyer meeting seller, and with nobody in between, where they can agree on a price, and you can run an exchange like Bill does. But you need some sort of human intervention when you find that there are all buyers and no sellers out there, or all sellers and no buyers, and that there is no way to dig in the weeds to find where those buyers and sellers are. To take a Darwinian approach, we will get to what optimal is. It works that way in NASDAQ. Why isn't it going to work in the NYSE listed stocks?

ARONSON: No one disagrees with that? Okay, panelists. You are now going to each be king. There are six kings up here. The hell with what the SEC recommends, or the NASD, or the Big Board. You are going to make a change in market structure. What is the most important change that you would make to accommodate best execution? What is the one thing that you would want to do, that would be first on your king agenda? Art, do you want to start?

HOGAN: Sure. God, I have always wanted to have that question. If you look at the value proposition that both exchanges and the ECNs bring to bear on our marketplace and on market structure, one of the things that we have not talked about today – and that is addressed in Reg NMS – is how

---

[17] The Market Maker in the Age of the ECN, Wayne Wagner, *Journal of Investment Management*, 1st Quarter edition, 2004 (www.joim.com).

they actually make money. Making money is a combination of things for an exchange. ECNs make (correct me if I am wrong) a high percentage of their money charging access fees. But the ECNs also make money every time they print a trade, as does NASDAQ, as does the NYSE. The ability to print a trade in one venue versus another has caused competitive pressures. This has actually worked in the real world to bring prices down. But the Consolidated Tape Association revenues are clearly a major piece of the business proposition of running an exchange. I am sure that I will be corrected if I have this wrong.

That said, there is a failure right now to put a positive bias on the ability of exchanges to show quotes and/or add liquidity to the system. I am referring to real liquidity quotes that are accessible on an equal level. That is part of the response to what the SEC has said, it is a part of what is in Reg NMS. There should be a combination, or a hybrid, of not just paying market centers for printing trades, but also of paying them for showing liquidity, for giving free and equal access to liquidity. In the perfect world, competition would be driven by where one can actually go to get the contra side of a trade done. That would be my suggestion.

ARONSON: King Bill.

O'BRIEN: My wife is a doctor, so I am a strong believer in 'first, do no harm.' But there are a couple of things that I would do. On the point of market data, the current system is inefficient. The cost of market data is widely recognized to be too high. That being said, there is, thankfully, finally, some competitive pressures on the supply side to the extent that SROs are competing for the business to be the generators of market data. Those generators, by virtue of that revenue stream, are lowering their costs to their customers who are typically the net consumers of market data. Brut is a classic example of this. We started to use the National Stock Exchange in July of 2003, and we lowered our prices by 30 percent as a result of that new revenue stream. But to the extent that you want to revise that and make the competition lower costs more explicitly, try to do so in a way that does not dull competition. I am hesitant to have those formulas changed in a way that is more quote driven. I do not believe that market data plans should be like the Internal Revenue code, promoting on a social policy level what are good orders and what are not good orders.

A couple of issues need to be examined to determine whether or not there is a problem that needs fixing. First there are short sales. Either we need to have a short sale rule or we do not. Let's make a decision and stick with it. If you need a pilot period to amass data to make the decision, then I am all for it. Let's start tomorrow.

The second issue is locked and crossed markets. You at least must have a debate about whether a locked market is an appropriate action. If you view a quote as inaccessible, rather than trying to ship to and wait two or three minutes, you should just lock it. But if access issues are resolved, then we need to make a decision about locked and crossed markets. I think Reg NMS tried to do that. I tend towards being in favor of it.

I strongly believe that competitive market forces and the SRO structure can resolve most other issues, and that the 'king' should be more of an English style king and let the process work.

ARONSON: I am glad that you brought up short sales. I want to return to it in a minute, but first let me go down the panel. Dick.

ROSENBLATT: First, Ted, I would like to thank you. I like this idea of being king. About 50 years ago, Peter Drucker was writing about monopolies. He said that as soon as an alternative shows up, business is going to flow to that alternative because people do not like being forced to trade anywhere, even if the alternative is not as efficient as the perceived monopoly. I only mention that because, while I do not think that the New York Stock Exchange is a monopoly, it is perceived by many to be one. I do not think that we should focus too much on why the NYSE loses some of its order flow. It loses a small percentage of its non-block order flow to competing exchanges and ECNs. It loses some of its order flow because it feels good to do it elsewhere, not because its competitors provide better pricing or liquidity. You do not want to rebuild the NYSE structure around the assumptions that the ECNs have a better model for trading stocks. Certainly, the NYSE will benefit from enhanced technology, but its real edge seems to be that price discovery, volume discovery, providing meaningful liquidity, and disseminating real-time market information on institutional supply and demand are still best accomplished by humans.

Our markets are evolving. Our technological capabilities are evolving at an ever-increasing pace. For markets to be efficient, we have to make maximum use of those technological innovations and advances. Right now, price discovery, volume discovery, information flow and reacting to unexpected opportunities are handled far better by people than by computers. Also, the commitment of capital is a reactive event. I use Bobby Fagenson's specialist capital all day long. Not because he is standing there making a thousand share market. Yeah, I will use that. But, more importantly, I will make a suggestion, he will make a counter suggestion, he eventually might give me the liquidity that I need, and we create a trade. That is how it works.

Specialists put up their capital reacting to an opportunity. The specialists do not just put it up there waiting for somebody to pick them off. Computers still do not do that well. That is the beauty of the New York Stock Exchange. That said, the specialists still need to evolve. They need to incorporate more technology. Other systems will come along. It is America, so everybody is going to try to build a better mousetrap. But that mousetrap, by its nature, being electronic, is somewhat rigid.

That big, cumbersome, New York Stock Exchange is not really rigid at all. It has a manual system working side-by-side with an electronic system. When the electronics work better, it will either incorporate those electronics or it will lose its order flow. One of the beauties of technology is that it has made order flow much more mobile. Primary market status is still important. But every week it becomes less important.

So, as king, I would keep the pressure on everybody to be better. I would keep complaining about access. I am sure that Paul Davis and I would differ on some of the specifics of a virtual crowd, but I like the concept. I would make sure that we evaluate things based on what is best for us. But we should not get bogged down with the cliché that the New York Stock Exchange is anti-competitive. I have not heard anything that makes the New York Stock Exchange non-competitive. You can compete with the NYSE.

Do not get bogged down with the trade-through rule. It is not about that. It is about best price. All you want is the best price. So keep it simple. Demand that all of the market centers and all of the brokers, provide you with what you need today and tomorrow. Do not let them get stuck in the past even though it is safer to be there.

ARONSON: Lanny.

L. SCHWARTZ: I guess it may be an internal contradiction, but as king I would pick up on some of the libertarian themes I heard earlier from O'Brien and Nicoll. Where there is vigorous competition – the options market being the one that I am most familiar with –, get the government out of it to a greater degree. Where there are multiple markets willing to offer services, do not let the government's policy, either directly in a statute, or indirectly in the hands of the mandarins in Washington, dictate when and how quickly marketplaces can offer new services and increase their competitive advantages.

When the markets increase their competitive advantages, chances are the customers will benefit. I would put the exchanges and the ECNs on a more level playing field in terms of their ability to be nimble, to make changes in their market structure. I would go in the opposite direction from where the Commission is heading in trying to regulate access fees. I would have less government intervention with access fees than there is now. I would get rid of the short sale rule, unless it can be demonstrated in particular cases that it is helpful and important. That is what I would do.

ARONSON: Mike, any edicts from you?

SIMON: I am going to echo a lot of what Lanny said. I guess it is going against type as a lawyer and a regulator, but I would argue for letting the natural economic forces have more control than the SEC. The first thing I would do is withdraw Reg NMS. When you look at what is in there, it is a very troubling release. Not only does it criminalize trade-throughs, as Lanny says, it would also regulate access fees. We have not mentioned the market data formula. If anybody in this room understands it, please spend a couple of hours with me afterwards and explain it to me. If we do not understand it, they are going to make us have advisory committees that will advise us on what these formulas are. Not only are they criminalizing trade-throughs, but they are also criminalizing locked markets. A pattern or practice of locking markets will also be a disciplinary violation. How providing customers a zero spread in a stock or an option is a criminal activity alludes me. I think you would have to back off of Reg NMS, realize that the markets are not as broken as the SEC thinks, and have a little bit more faith in natural economic forces.

ARONSON: Wayne.

WAGNER: Rich Rosenblatt said that we must figure out what is best for us. That is not the question. The question is, what is best for the investing public. All transaction costs are negative performance. They all hurt investors, and they hurt the economy as a whole. We have been arguing a lot about whose ox is going to get gored where I see the inefficiencies in the market. All you have to do is to look at error rates on trades here and see how drastically they have come down. It used to be around six percent on manual trades. It's effectively zero with today's completed electronic trades. And you say that all this stuff is really good, it is making the entire process

CHAPTER 5: ELECTRONIC TRADING

Moderator– Matthew Andresen
Former CEO, Island
Board of Directors, Lava Trading
George Bodine, General Motors Investment Management Corporation
Director of Trading
Christopher Concannon, The NASDAQ Stock Market
Executive Vice President, Transaction Services
Richard Korhammer, Lava Trading Inc.
Chairman & Chief Executive Officer
Michael LaBranche, LaBranche & Company
Chairman, Chief Executive Officer and President
Brett Redfearn, American Stock Exchange
Senior Vice President, Business Strategy and Equity Order Flow

MATTHEW ANDRESEN: I do not know how many at this conference are as deeply ingrained in this subject as I am but, believe it or not, the floor community and the electronic community do not always see eye to eye on all issues (laughter). So, to get to the bottom of this shocking discovery, we have assembled an all-star panel of different constituencies. We are fortunate to have George Bodine here representing the big buy-side players. We have Chris Concannon representing NASDAQ, and Rich Korhammer from Lava representing the technology firms, the aggregators. We have Michael LaBranche, CEO of the largest specialist firm on the New

York Stock Exchange. And we have Brett Redfearn from the American Stock Exchange. Let's jump right into it.

We will not hear any canned speeches. We will go right into the Q and A. I have a list of questions, but it will be most helpful if you in the crowd jump in and ask some questions as well.

Rich Korhammer, I will start with you. As the one player up here who is in the business of serving the sell-side[18] directly with technology products that span across marketplaces, what does Lava hear in this debate about floor versus electronic trading? Does it matter to you as an aggregator what the market structure for a particular destination is?

RICHARD KORHAMMER: Fundamentally, as a technology provider, our job is to help customers trade within whatever market structure the SEC, the broker dealers, and the investment community put together. At the same time, we see certain rules or proposed structures that may not be fluid, that may cause problems in the marketplace. That will no doubt be part of our discussion. But, as a neutral technology provider, our job is to link markets together, listed or NASDAQ. We may try to stay out of the fray as it relates to some of these issues. But we will get involved in the debate.

ANDRESEN: George Bodine, everyone seems to care deeply about you because everything we hear has to do with what is best for the institutional investor. But we do not often hear directly from the horse's mouth. As a buy-side trader, given the challenges that you face managing the enormous sums of money under your control, what motivates you when you are trying to get an execution done? What are the most important factors for you?

GEORGE BODINE: I have tried to consider the advantages of electronic over floor-based trading. And it has always mystified me. I trade a lot of instruments throughout the world. One of the most active is the S&P futures. The futures market is probably where we have the best example of

---

[18] Lava, a wholly-owned independent subsidiary of Citigroup, can be used by both the buy-side as well as the sell-side. However, buy-side customers must be 'sponsored' by a member of the sell-side to utilize the services of Lava, an electronic system regarded as a direct market access provider. Lava says it has business relationships with the top Wall Street brokerage firms and many smaller firms. It also indirectly services institutional customers, including hedge funds. Lava's success can be traced to its introduction of ColorBook in 1999, an ECN aggregator that combined all of the books of the major NASDAQ trading venues out of a fragmented marketplace.

human interaction in the trading markets. It is where we have a pit process with everyone trading the same instruments. It is not an auction market, but it is an open outcry system, and you have all the bodies there. However, if you look at the e-mini,[19] which trades the same S&P 500 futures contract one-fifth the size, it is more costly to trade the e-mini when you compare the notional amount from a commission standpoint. It takes five of those e-minis for every one of the large contracts that I want to trade, to invest the same dollar amount. And yet, the volume has surged. I think it now represents nearly 60 to 70 percent of the day's notional trading volume in S&P 500 futures contracts on the CME. This e-mini, which trades electronically, has done extremely well. I ask, why is this happening?

We are having this argument today about electronic versus the floor, and it really puzzles me because it seems clear that electronic trading is a superior model. In some cases, in the less liquid stocks, for instance, you need some human intervention. But most of the traders I know on the institutional side want control of their orders. They want immediacy and anonymity and they will gravitate to the venue, that provides it.

Unfortunately, when you trade on a floor-based system, there is a relinquishing of this control. You have delegated the trade, you have subcontracted it out, and there is a critical 30-second to three-minute window when you go through all the angst of trying to figure out, 'Was it broken up, did I get it all, was there stock ahead?' A lot of institutions do not like to go through that. We want immediacy. We want to get the job done so that we can move on. As for anonymity, many people have made a lot of money front running a lot of institutional orders. Therefore, the venue that provides anonymity is the one that will attract the most activity.

ANDRESEN: Michael, how would you articulate the core strength of the specialist market? Can you see a way to duplicate the advantages of the specialist system in a more electronic format? What are those advantages, and can they be delivered in a different context?

MICHAEL LaBRANCHE: I could be here all day talking about that. There are a couple of interesting things going on. The International Securities Exchange (ISE), for example, uses a specialist system, and the ISE is an electronic market. But the most important thing to consider is the

---

[19] An e-mini is an electronically traded futures contract – such as the e-mini S&P 500 – which is denominated in smaller sizes than the standard contract. The Chicago Mercantile's e-minis were launched in 1997 for retail investors, but institutions have now become active traders in e-minis.

auction, which protects the public. Look at what has happened. There has been a lot of focus on execution quality and fairness in the market while the ISE is bringing an auction to an electronic market for the first time. It is an untested concept, but you can certainly understand why it is going there. The ISE wants the market to price something.

Think about what the auction does. The specialist at the NYSE is just one piece of the puzzle. We happen to manage the auction, but the product that we have is the fairness and transparency of the pricing. We want to offer more products and anonymity. We are taking the best element of the auction, which is liquidity. We are going to meld those with other technologies when we go to a fast market, for example. In the future, you will see more points of sales being linked directly to the ultimate customer. As you get more linkage, people will have more control. You are not going to have that three-minute window that George is referring to; where you think that you do not have control over the order. You will be able to autoex whatever the displayed liquidity is, with the NYSE moving to a fast market. This means that we will be on a first-come, first-served basis. The first person to press a button will get what is there. They will get it without the fear of someone in the crowd trading ahead of them. And these are all positive developments.

What Rich Korhammer is doing with his business is very interesting. He is becoming an aggregator of liquidity. He is finding all the venues. When we talk about ECNs, we talk about new products. They will all work together.

What does the specialist and the New York Stock Exchange do? We are just a destination, one of many destinations. We happen to be a big destination. We will be linked through ECNs, ultimately through products at the front end, and through what Lava does. You will see a lot of changes there.

ANDRESEN: Brett, please continue with that thought. What is your vision of a hybrid marketplace? Is it mixing the floor with the electronic?

BRETT REDFEARN: We are spending a lot of time drilling down and looking at new systems. Reg NMS and the SEC have definitely sparked the exchanges to bring more automation into the marketplace. We sat down and said, 'Okay, we need to become more electronic. We want to have the inside bid and offer automatically executed. But how do we do some of the things that Michael LaBranche was talking about in terms of maintaining the benefits of the specialist system? There are very distinct differences between the way the auction market and the dealer market operates. Specialists have stabilization requirements; they have obligations to be buyers and sellers of last resort. When the market is heading down, they will be there to buy. When the market is heading up, they will be there to sell. There are some real benefits to the auction market that actually protect against the ImClone's in the market. As you may recall, on February 14th, 2004, ImClone – IMCL – stock dropped $6.50, over 16%, in less than two minutes, based upon what appeared to be a bad rumor with no mechanism in the market to protect against such excessive volatility.

So, how do you integrate stabilizing features into an automated auction market system? How, in a fully automated environment, is the specialist incented to play this role? Because if you remove that role and, if you make the auction market too much like the dealer market, you lose the differentiation – and benefits – of the auction market. And this could actually destabilize the market. In many respects, we think that the stabilization function, the balance in the market, is a good thing. And we want to continue this feature to differentiate ourselves.

ANDRESEN: Brett, will that distinction be made on a product-by-product basis? George Bodine always talks about how, in some securities, there is simply no need for any intervention or stabilization, whether it be Microsoft, or Hewlett Packard, or the Qs. What do you guys at the AMEX think about segmenting by product in terms of how much electronic business you do?

REDFEARN: As surprising as this may seem, we do not have a full consensus on that question yet. There are people who believe that one standard should apply to all securities. Some of the questions we are thinking about right now include: at what point does an order come to the floor and result in an imbalance so large that you should stop the market? If a stock typically trades about 100,000 shares a day and a 50,000-share order is entered into the system, should we simply allow that order to rip through the order book unchecked, knowing that would bang the stock down 15 percent in two minutes? How should we handle that particular type of situation? Should triggers be built into an electronic system so that, if the market moves too fast in too short a period of time, it could actually be slowed down or stopped? A runaway market situation is not a good thing, even if only in one security.

A lot of different possibilities are being tossed around right now. Sixty percent of all of the stocks in the marketplace – that's all stocks traded at the New York Stock Exchange, the NASDAQ National Market, and in the

AMEX – trade less that 100,000 shares a day, on average. While we have learned some important things from the behavior of the QQQ and from Microsoft and Cisco, these lessons do not necessarily apply to all of the securities in the market. Less liquid securities behave differently from highly liquid securities. If we try to apply the same thinking to all types of securities, we will create problems in areas that we are not yet thinking about.

ANDRESEN: Chris, I need to ask you the next question. But before we get to your market structure question, I must ask, what is up with these new price cuts? This is not the NASDAQ that I remember. Frankly, I would like to know why these cuts were not made when I could really have benefited from them.

CHRISTOPHER CONCANNON: I think you did benefit from the old model. Let me start with a brief history. We have spent the last eight months focused on internal costs and internal structures. NASDAQ had a lot of costs, whether it was NASDAQ Europe, or new products that NASDAQ was trying to roll out. We cut those costs. We took out products, we took out services, and we eliminated a lot of costs. In fact, at the end of the year, we had eliminated over a hundred million dollars in run rate costs. Entering into '04, our plan was to have a clear path to continue to reduce costs.

ANDRESEN: Sounds like you would be fun to work for.

CONCANNON: Yeah. I was fun to work for. Actually, we had that plan in place entering into '04 with the mindset that we would be a price leader. We have what I would call enterprise risk. We have listing business and data business. These very valuable businesses are at risk if we do not succeed. So we are the most committed party in the space. We now have the cost structure to be the price leader, and we just took action.[20]

ANDRESEN: Okay. Now, how do you respond to Michael LaBranche and Brett Redfearn's comments about the floor-based market? When you are at NASDAQ, how do you view their space? How do you seek to challenge the New York Stock Exchange's supremacy in those stocks? How about touching on dual listing and other things that you guys have tried to do?

---

[20] In other words, NASDAQ reduced costs, made cuts in various areas to position itself as the low-cost provider among other execution players in transactions for dealers and other participants.

CONCANNON: I am encouraged that everyone is talking more electronics and not less. Clearly, no one is asking NASDAQ to introduce a floor model. They are headed in our direction. That is a direction that we have been playing in for quite some time. We know it well. We have gotten our costs in line, and we know the difficulties of participating in the fully automated space.

I do worry about the floor model. We can define the differences in terms of the access point for investors – floor versus electronic. On the floor, there are not too many individual investors being represented by floor brokers getting the point of sale advantage. Can you deliver that in a hybrid model? I have not seen it. I see hybrid models where only the institutions benefit from the hybrid portion, and not the fully automated portion. As the NYSE talks about moving to a hybrid approach, I hope that the individual investor gets the same benefits that an institutional investor would get. I look at the differences between the floor model and the fully electronic model, and I think about the individual investor who, in the electronic model, has the same access that George Bodine has on his desktop. They are both looking at the same screen. They have the same rights to the quotes that they are trying to access. That is a better playing field. It certainly attracts more liquidity when you consider the volumes that the fully electronic markets do. That is all good.

On the issue of volatility and a large imbalance coming down the floor, I worry about the discretion that a floor model hands the specialist. The specialists have to decide whether this is true price discovery. Someone put that order in because they think it is the right price. The specialist has the discretion to decide whether to stop the market from moving. He can give people time to react. But I worry about when you hand someone the discretion to determine the true price. You do not have that discretion in the electronic markets. You have people who need to know where their own prices should be set, and they trade at those pricing levels. They execute at those pricing levels. It is the discretion that I worry about.

ANDRESEN: You are clearly a moderator's best friend. That was quite an answer. Rich Korhammer, you are someone who has built a business around accessing pools of liquidity or, as Michael LaBranche has put it, accessing the destination. I am most impressed that we have gone 30 minutes without talking about the trade-through rule. What I am always interested to hear you talk about is the differences between trading in parallel and trading-through. Maybe we can have George Bodine's opinion on that as well when you are done. Perhaps you can talk about how you define these two things, and about what the differences are.

KORHAMMER: Sure. But before I do, I want to say that there are two important differences between a floor-based model and an electronic venue. It is not to say that one is better than the other. They are different. It goes back to the traders' choice of where their orders will best be represented. The first difference is that, in the floor-based model, the person removing liquidity has the potential benefit of getting a better price (i.e., price improvement). That is an interesting dynamic that many investors enjoy. The second difference is that a person who has added liquidity in a floor-based model may not get that particular trade done because someone else might be able to get it by introducing a better price. In an electronic model, when someone adds an order that becomes visible in the marketplace, that market center will more or less make sure that that bid is hit, or that the offer is taken. Traders are choosing which model may make more sense for them, and there are pretty big differences. We will continue to see that level of competition over time.

People are talking about trading-through versus trading parallel. There are pretty big differences. Our technologies, for example, are not really designed to trade-through. What our technologies, and other similar technologies are doing, is trading in parallel. For example, let us say that we have a two bid by four offer marketplace. There might be a couple of fours, there might be a couple of fives, and there might be a couple of sixes. What happens if I go after 50,000 shares to buy in the four, five and six range together, in parallel? What does that mean from the implications of trade-through? Perhaps the NYSE is sitting on four right now. If I send all the shares that are displayed on the NYSE, and simultaneously send out orders to other market centers in four, five and six, have I traded through? I think that the answer is 'no.' I would not be trading through because I am trading in parallel.

When we overlay that against the regulatory changes being considered, what obligation does a market center have if the market center's best offer is five? Should they wait until they see that the four is cleared if they are concerned that maybe they permitted a trade-through to occur? Does the market center have the obligation to say, 'wait a second'? If so, I cannot trade. I am going to hold this order, and thus not allow trading to take place. Or, are there vehicles where someone (a broker, for example) could say, 'Do not worry. I know that you see that there is a four out there, and I am sending you a five. I have already sent an order to that four.'

One of the ways that trading-through versus trading in parallel is handled is with a 'pre-comply.' This is the term used in a situation where a trader transacts a trade simultaneously at multiple price points without violating regulations in trading through a better price. It works like this: A pre-comply flag is sent by the broker via an order management system. The message will be sent, usually by FIX, to a market center and be tagged 'pre-comply.' This instructs the market center to continue the trade with the broker who sent the pre-comply, and it permits the market center to ignore superior prices it might see. In effect, the broker is essentially telling the market center that the broker will assume responsibility for best execution and trade-through obligations. In this situation, the broker will send simultaneous order requests to all necessary and better prices in the overall market rather than the one the market center is offering. A lot of volume could trade quickly while making sure that no one has traded through, either a small investor or a large investor.

ANDRESEN: George, the proliferation of tools and technology products that have been made available to the market centers have evolved in terms of added new features and benefits. Given that much regulation is focused on retail investors and individual retail execution quality, as someone who has large orders to get done, have you found any negative impacts from the proliferation of electronic tools?

BODINE: I would like to address trade-through first. We have been doing this for every block trade that we do. It is usually negotiated upstairs. You get a set of alternative prices, to buy it up a quarter or up seven cents for this, or up 15 cents for this, or up 20 cents for this large amount. At that juncture, we have essentially traded through. We have made a determination that we are willing to pay through whatever prices were down there, because we feel that we understand where supply and demand is. Institutional traders use the mental process of trade-through on a regular basis. It seems to me that the trade-through rule is geared for smaller size orders rather than for the larger institutional order.

As for electronic tools, I have been involved in both the New York's ITAC and NASDAQ's ITAC groups.[21] I do not have any bias one way or the other. But I work for General Motors Asset Management, and we oversee in excess of 120 billion, of which we manage less than 20 percent internally. We have, I would say, 55 to 60 outside managers. When we

---

[21] ITAC is the acronym for Institutional Trading Advisory Committee at the NYSE. At NASDAQ, it is the Institutional Trading Advisory Council.

terminate a manager and hire a new manager, we take those assets in-house and handle the transition ourselves. There are four of us on the desk, and we will handle a half a billion to a billion dollars within a couple of days.

The electronic efficiencies that are afforded out there through the various venues have been a phenomenal boon for us. We would not have been able to handle this through a floor-based model without these electronic efficiencies. And we do it seamlessly. Only a minimal number of trading errors have come in, and the executions are being done fairly reasonably, I think.

The comment was made earlier today that, if anyone does VWAP, they are really not doing their job. Unfortunately, when I give an assignment to do a VWAP trade and try to beat it, my success ratio, using the major firms, has been about two out of ten. So typically two times out of ten, these firms will beat the VWAP but on the eight other efforts they will either match VWAP or miss it. I find that VWAP is a very difficult measure to beat on a consistent basis.

The electronic efficiencies and the electronic capabilities that have come into the market in the last three or four years have made huge movements of dollar assets very easy for me. And I have not had to increase my trader complement by two or three people to handle that.

ANDRESEN: Michael, you obviously are a major player down at the New York Stock Exchange. What are you pushing the exchange to do that will make your job easier as a specialist? Anything like what technology has done for George's business?

LaBRANCHE: One of the big misconceptions about the floor and the specialist industry in particular is that, somehow or other, our interests run counter to increased technology. That is absolutely not the case. People say that our market is the manual market. It is not. Today, ninety-nine percent of the orders are transmitted as messages to the point of sale. That is up from zero percent in 1977.

We are a liquidity provider that is increasingly linked electronically to customers. We were the pioneer in delivering that, using our DOT system. We think that more technology will be inevitable. This does not run counter to having a specialist system or an auction. Last year, our company received 110 million market orders. The orders were delivered to us, and they ranged in size from 110 shares to three million shares each. Those orders were sent to us voluntarily. No one said that they had to be sent to us. They could have gone to other places. The reason why we got 110 million orders in a year is presumably because people have liked the experience in the past.

They are willing to send us more orders. The critical element has got to be customer satisfaction.

Going back to what George Bodine said, there are certain things that need to be done in our market. I would stress that one of the most important is the increased links to the ultimate customer. There is no reason to think that technology, floor-based systems, liquidity, and capital cannot all be tied together.

ANDRESEN: Brett, what about the AMEX?

REDFEARN: We are making significant investments in technology. Right now we are looking at a lot of opportunities to integrate specialists into a much more automated floor-based auction market. We also pay close attention to our issuers – the companies that list on our exchange. As you know, we do not just compete for trading, we also compete for listings. You would really be surprised by how many of the issuers that transfer to the Amex from NASDAQ say to us, 'we did not like the volatility that we had in that other market. We did not like how the prices moved around so much.'

The issuers are an important constituency not often included in this debate. When CEOs of companies come to us and complain about excessive volatility, we are concerned about how much volatility is too much volatility. When we think about the design of the future automated trading systems, as I mentioned before, we do not want to have ImClone situations, where a stock's price moves too far too fast.

We also worry about how fast is too fast. We looked at a few stocks in the NASDAQ market this last Friday. We saw situations where there were 25 quote updates per second. People really have to start asking, how many quote updates a second are too many? How many transaction price changes in the same second are too many?

I can show you an example where stocks were printing to the tape 25 cents apart in the same second. Is that helping the market? We try to find the balance between moving toward more electronic trading and providing more certainty, and at the same time not degrading the market quality that we offer our issuers and investors.

ANDRESEN: Chris, how do you respond to that, to the hemorrhaging of listing for volatility and stuff like that?

CONCANNON: We certainly care about our issuers. We spend a lot of time talking about volatility. There is a big debate about volatility and the differences between the two markets. I have to start out by saying that I would like to see your volatility after you have become a so-called fast market. There are substantial changes to the model. The volatility results when you actually have autoex on the quote. When you are a fast market, the stock moves faster.

But back to Brett's question, 'How fast is too fast?' I do not know how we answer that. We give people through the market the tools to decide how fast is too fast. Rather than having a human decide for them what speed this stock should trade at, and the price at which it should trade. The volatility is interesting though. We have looked at volatility. The New York did a volatility study of stocks that switched from NASDAQ to New York and, for the large stocks captured in that study, the volatility actually increased.[22] But for the small stocks, which probably trade under 100,000 shares, the volatility decreased.

You have to look at those small stocks. Our dealers are subject to autoex on the quote. So there is a difference in trading patterns between a fast market and a slow market. You cannot have the volatility debate without talking about the quality of execution that your market delivers, and about the speed of execution.

For intra-day volatility (the price swings within a given day) there are absolute differences between the two models. For inter-day, where the price ends up over time, the volatility numbers are identical. One question is, how do we restrict intraday price moves? Another question is, should we be restricting it? If someone has a price point that they want to trade at, who am I to say that they cannot trade there? I would rather let the market decide. Let the market make up its mind about what the true price is at any given time. I just cannot imagine trying to stop quote updates. Those are limit orders trying to be displayed. To suggest that we should restrict the prices from being disseminated runs counter to every regulation that has been issued over the past 20 years. I do not see us restricting quote updates.

ANDRESEN: Chris, can you view the market experiment with sub-pennies to be a sort of …. Which of you guys would take that as an example of things working right now? You know, the ECNs moved forward to quoting and transacting in increments of less than a penny. They had an initial success, and then they subsequently found that there were deleterious effects to their liquidity and to people's happiness with their system. They

---

[22] See Research Papers on NYSE.com: Market Structure, Fragmentation and Market Quality: Evidence from Recent Listing Switches by Paul Bennett and Li Wei. Paper #: 2003-04. As of June 2005, the study was still in the publication process. The study examines 39 stocks, comparing medium- and small-cap with large cap on the NYSE.

voluntarily started truncating their decimal places back to full pennies. Would you consider that a market solution of people trying to see if it goes too far? Or is Brett right that sometimes there is a bridge too far?[23]

CONCANNON: That is an example where Brett would be right.

ROBERT WOOD (University of Memphis) [From the Floor]: I have a quick comment on the comparative studies of volatility between the NYSE and NASDAQ. It is really hard to get a clean read on the data from NASDAQ because NASDAQ dealers have up to 90 seconds to report a trade That means the sequence of the trades reported may not be in order, tick by tick.[24] It is my understanding that a significant amount of the liquidity in NASDAQ is now offered by SOES bandit firms, that the traditional market makers are out of that space in terms of providing liquidity.[25] This can happen because these SOES bandit types are not regulated like market makers. They have no SEC oversight, they have no affirmative obligation, so their costs are going to be inherently lower. What is worrisome, given the sophisticated algorithms they are using to place limit orders, is that the minute you want them in there they are gone. The minute the market moves against them, they step aside. This is particularly true in the less liquid stocks. This can lead to these volatility problems. I am curious about what the implications of this are in terms of the nature of the market, and the nature of regulation. Is this inevitable when we go fully electronic?

ANDRESEN: Chris.

---

[23] The 'bridge too far' is a metaphorical reference to Operation Market Garden in World War II. Andresen made it to question the benefits of finer trading increments. As he later explained, Operation Market Garden was a 'bold, silly and tragic' plan by British Gen. Montgomery to parachute thousands of Allied troops behind German lines in Holland. 'As it turned out, Montgomery was famously a 'bridge too far' in his plans,' Andresen said. 'The unfortunate group protecting the Arnheim bridges were left for over a week instead of the planned three days, waiting for relief from the main Allied forces.' Similarly, the movement towards finer trading increments initially had a positive outcome, according to Andresen. However, the ECNs discovered that moving towards even finer increments had a deleterious effect on liquidity.

[24] NASD rules generally require a member, during normal market hours, to report securities transactions within 90 seconds after each execution.

[25] At the time of this conference, there was evidence of a growing popularity of black box style trading, which used sophisticated strategies in NASDAQ trading. The players reportedly accounted for a large proportion of NASDAQ liquidity. They included Lime Brokerage, Wedbush Morgan and Trillium Trading, a successor firm of SOES trading brokerage DATEK Online.

CONCANNON: I think you called them SOES bandit firms. I have not seen one of those since…

WOOD: SOES bandit firms. They stopped making money about '99 or so. But several of them stayed in the business, so they are now essentially in the business of market making.

CONCANNON: One phenomenon that I saw in the day trading community over the last two years is that they actually switched from trading a majority of NASDAQ stocks to trading a majority of NYSE stocks. You did see the day traders actually change the floor model despite what we are talking about up here as the different models.

Who are the liquidity providers in NASDAQ? It is still the traditional large firms, market makers, and dealers who are providing liquidity. You will find in the ECNs that there are what I would call the black box or program trading firms that are providing liquidity in the top 100 stocks. They are not in the small stocks at all. They live off of volatility, or they live off of liquidity and transaction volume. They thrive in the larger stocks where the market has accepted them and actually welcomes the liquidity they provide.

I do not know about their quotes being fleeting quotes. I mean, there are live orders, and when you look at the activity levels that they reach, and the level of added volume that they put into the system, they are valuable players in our securities markets. To ignore them or to do anything to damage their model is not the direction to go.

Your point is a good one. We should be concerned about these purely electronic market makers. What are their obligations at the end of the day? We think about that a lot at NASDAQ. We hold our market makers to a standard. All the time, there must be a two-sided quote. That is not a requirement of these firms inside the ECNs.

ANDRESEN: Michael, as you noted, you are effectively a market maker. You are making a market within the context of this larger marketplace. Do you ever think about being in the market making business in an over-the-counter environment, or in an electronic environment? Is this something that ever crosses your mind?

LaBRANCHE: We do this. It is a different division. Obviously, the business in the over-the-counter market has changed dramatically. Our business is changing too. There is a whole different world out there – decimals, more electronics, people slicing orders up, people trying to beat the VWAP, and people hiding as closet indexers and all that kind of stuff. We can talk all day about what is the better thing, about whether or not you should have a floor. Ultimately, orders will find their way to the best market. They will go to where they will get the best return, the best price, and the most money back. It is that simple.

Rich Korhammer's technology will find that market. You can ring a bell on the podium or stand in front of the NASDAQ market, but it will not make a difference. Ultimately, what matters is where people get the best prices. At the New York Stock Exchange, our market share is hanging right in there at 80 percent. When we went public in '99, the analyst who covered us said that our market share would be 70 percent in five years. But it is not. It all depends on where the best price is given. The reason why people are not making markets in the over-the-counter market is because it does not pay anymore. That is what happened.

ANDRESEN: Benn.

BENN STEIL (Council on Foreign Relations) [From the Floor]: Michael, if I heard you correctly, you said that last year you received 110 million orders, and that all of these orders were sent 'voluntarily.' If that is the case, am I right in saying that, as a matter of your personal business interest, you are wholly relaxed about the potential elimination of the trade-through rule?

LaBRANCHE: Am I wholly relaxed about it? Can I be partially relaxed? Or a little bit relaxed, or a little uptight about it (laughter)? I think that George described something very interesting. The trade-through rule is more of a public policy issue. The most important thing is for the public to think that their brokers are finding them the best prices, no matter what. The important thing is that brokers be held to that fiduciary responsibility. If people (especially retail investors) start to get the impression that their orders are being arbitraged by their own broker, or by someone who works for their broker, or by someone who has an arrangement with their broker, that will ultimately be harmful to the market psychology. Because the U.S. capital markets, especially the equity markets, are the most efficient markets, they are the ones where people go to try and get the best price. I can tell you that trading on the NASDAQ and the New York Stock Exchange is much better than trading in London. That is because there is this policy of having a trade-through rule. This means that you are always trying to find the best price.

Philosophically, I think that it is very important to keep the rule. Would it really affect us that much if the rule was not there? Its absence would affect us if the psychology of the market got damaged. If people did not want to use the market anymore, then its absence would affect us. That is the key issue here.

REDFEARN: I would say that there has always been the notion that, if market participants can access the best price, they will. There are some circumstances under which this principal is not true. There are option strategies where it might not make sense to hit the best price. There are situations where, if you have a one or a two-cent de minimus trade-through exception, this facilitates the profitability of a particular internalization model. There are upstairs facilitation orders where a firm might want to be on the other side of a large block order. In fact, in many cases, this happens today. You have non-ITS CAES market participants and, if the order size is over 10,000 shares, they can be on the other side of the cross and not get broken up; whereas if they go to the floor and receive price improvement, they will get broken up

There are different examples of ways in which market participants can avoid the trade-through rule. In fact, there are incentives not to abide by the trade-through rule. This raises questions about fundamental market integrity. Today, people are debating this issue in terms of differing market models where one market model is fast and accessible and another market is slow and less accessible. Presumably there will be much more automation and a much greater ability to automatically access the inside quote at all markets in the near future. Generally speaking, the majority of people out there believe that, once the access problem is solved – for example, automated and certain access – , most will feel good about maintaining that particular rule.

ANDRESEN: Rich, your company allows us to solve this problem independently of regulation-based solutions. Is there still a need for regulation in this matter? Or is the problem of finding the best price solved by having ever more efficient destinations, and by having someone be your personal shopper to get the best price?

LaBRANCHE: There are some fundamental questions about what controls are currently in place, and what 'after the fact' vehicles exist to determine if someone was or was not following best execution practices. The equities marketplace is fairly transparent. Prints are going off every 90 seconds. They can be reviewed to see if someone was printing away from the inside, or if there was a pattern of abuse. The bigger question that we bring to the forefront is what are the costs and benefits of implementing 50 different sets of rules versus being able to catch people after the fact. That is a cost- benefit analysis. These discussions make a lot of sense but, economically, what is the cost associated with implementing these solutions?

ANDRESEN: George, where do you come down on that?

BODINE: Why do not you rephrase the question?

ANDRESEN: Well, we are talking about the trade-through rule, and about whether the marketplace itself should have the obligation to rout out the problem. Or, should companies like Lava solve that problem? Is trade-through an issue that you worry about?

BODINE: No, I do not. I will worry about it if it becomes a legal problem and if I am violating something. But some of the proposals that have been set forth (the opt out rule and other things) will be totally cumbersome. Administratively, they will create a big burden.

ANDRESEN: So your concerns are more about the regulatory overhang and the cost associated with that?

BODINE: One of the big questions that comes up is, whose market data are we talking about? Are we talking about the market data that NASDAQ sees at this point in time? If you were to time it for a microsecond and have different marketplaces say, 'this is the market data that I see right now,' the NYSE will say one thing. But, if you go to Archipelago, they may have a different set of market data points at the exact same point in time, simply based on how quickly market data are transmitted and on how long it takes for the computer systems to register. So what is the market data? That goes back to the question of, when is a trade-through occurring? Is there a referee who says that this is the market data? Or, is the broker responsible for determining what they see, based on the vendor that they are using and their sets of market data? I do not think that these questions, or costs, or issues have been brought to the forefront. I do not think that the details have been thought about yet. These are some questions that will have to come out. You cannot implement solutions without addressing questions about whose market data we are talking about as it relates to trade-through.

REDFEARN: That is a function, again, of the fast market. If you have 20 quote updates a second, what are you going to hit? What is the quote that you are trying to get? The more quote updates that you have, the harder it is to know if you are trading through a market. That is where quote duration time will become increasingly important. Best execution will become harder and harder to measure if you have ten different quotes in the same second.

ANDRESEN: Question here?

PAUL DAVIS (TIAA-CREF) [From the Floor]: A definitional question for Michael or Brett. You used the phrase auction over and over again. Could you explain exactly what you mean by an auction over the normal course of events on the exchange? Is it an auction or is it just negotiations?

LeBRANCHE: No, it is an auction. A lot of people confuse the auction with someone yelling and screaming. The auction is not that. The auction is what allows the highest price to buy, and the lowest price to sell, at any given time. It does not discriminate based on size. A 100-share order gets the same benefit from the auction as a million-share order because there is an exposed bid and an exposed offer.

A Dutch auction, on the other hand, is one single event. It is one trade. It is a different kind of auction. Ours is a continuous, two-way auction, which is unique.

REDFEARN: I would add to that. It is liquidity aggregating at a point in time. One of the most obvious examples of that is the closing process on the exchange floor. We have learned that, if you have closing orders, they can come together at the end of the day. We can match up the buy-side and the sell-side, pair off imbalances, and put up something rational that gives meaningful price discovery, something that helps fill those orders. This results in a lot less price movement, and a lot fewer occurrences of prices whipping around the market and not participating in the official close.

ANDRESEN: We have someone here who knows something about call markets.

ROBERT SCHWARTZ (Baruch College) [From the Floor]: I just wanted further clarification. Would you call a continuous limit order platform an auction market?

CONCANNON: No. I would call that a staccato call market. It would be a series of call markets. A continuous auction is one where there is price discovery, and market orders are where you get price discovery. By definition, you need market orders for price discovery.

SCHWARTZ: But also the flexible handling of smart limit orders and NH orders.

CONCANNON: Marketable limit orders are a form of market order. When you talk about a fast market, if the quotes are 49.95 bid, 50.00 offered, 50,000 shares up, there is no price discovery for that amount of stock. You know that you can buy 50,000 at 50, you know that you can sell 50,000 at 49.95. Where price discovery occurs is when an order hits the market for a larger amount than the displayed liquidity. For example, if 300,000 come in to buy at market when only 50,000 shares are there to sell. Now you have price discovery on 250,000 because the market does not know what that is yet. That is where the continuous auction comes in.

SCHWARTZ: So the key is price discovery?

CONCANNON: Price discovery is the great benefit that you get from a continuous auction.

ANDRESEN: Another question?

WAYNE WAGNER (Plexus Group) [From the Floor]: Does not the resolution depend on whether the price comes back or not? If it goes down 25 percent and, at the next tick, it is back up to where it was, then it was a liquidity event, not a repricing of the asset.

REDFEARN: Would you want to be the seller down 25 percent based on a bad rumor? There are many situations where the specialists are buying on the way down to protect against that sort of volatile impact. We believe in protecting against that sort of market impact by stabilizing the price. Our provision of liquidity is a benefit to the market system. It is something that distinguishes the auction market from the dealer market.

WAGNER: I am trying to offer you an answer, and you won't take it.

REDFEARN: OK, I will jump on that one, Wayne. It sounds like a liquidity dislocation.

WAGNER: Yes, there is a time when you want to stop it.

REDFEARN: Would you want to buy at the opening of PLMO on NASDAQ when it went public?[26] You can pay 80 and then the next minute it is trading at 60. Yesterday on the Amex, we put up a million-share close in a NASDAQ stock called Sienna. This was done as part of our program with Standard & Poor's. We offset a million shares. We published the imbalances and, in so doing, largely offset the market imbalance. The specialist stood up and provided capital. He basically printed a million-share close in a stock that is associated with an index change right on the market. It was literally right on the market. These 200,000-share market-on-close orders we were receiving were not running into the market. They were not dramatically moving the price an excessive amount in one particular direction, and the system worked very well.

ANDRESEN: Brett, isn't this really a question of trade-offs? I think that everyone, even our electronic colleagues, would agree that a

---

[26] The initial public offering of palmOne (NASDAQ: PLMO) occurred on March 2, 2000.

situation like COCO would be hard to happen on the AMEX or the New York. But those are two situations out of 6,000 stocks in roughly five years. That is a relatively small number of events. In both cases, I believe that the trades were all broken anyway. It was embarrassing for NASDAQ with the issuer, I suppose, but it was quickly resolved.

How do you respond to Chris' point that it is fine to get that protection, but at what costs? There is still a cost for the people who need the immediacy. There is a little cost to having a slower market. That little cost is in the form of little nickels every day versus saving a dollar every once in a while.

REDFEARN: We have actually gone from looking at intraday volatility, to intra-minute volatility, to intra-second volatility. You can see trades hitting the tape 25 cents apart in a single second. When looking at intra-second volatility, at some point you have to question the quality of the market that is moving with such speed, with everything getting divvied up into microseconds.

Intra-second volatility, when it is really moving across the chart, is clearly not reflective of good price discovery. Multiple prices in one second? Multiple quotes in one second? At some point, this has gone too far. We talked before about what market structure is benefiting institutions and professional traders, and about what structure is benefiting retail traders. I do not think that the retail trader who is coming in through E*trade, Ameritrade, or some other online broker has a chance of getting that price in a millisecond. A professional trader will get it. You can have a situation where someone finds that they were 'traded ahead' on the NYSE because the execution took ten seconds, but you can also have a situation where somebody else traded ahead of you because he or she could execute in ten milliseconds.

ANDRESEN: A question there?

WILLIAM FREUND (Pace University) [From the Floor]: I have a question for Mike. You have talked about the hybrid market that is about to emerge on the New York Stock Exchange. Can you give us some clarification about whether the customer will determine whether an order goes to an automated exchange or to an auction market? Will there be some interaction between these two markets?

LaBRANCHE: I do not think that there will be a separate automated exchange per se. The words 'hybrid market' are being overused at this point. The hybrid really is a transition. It is a natural extension of the DOT system. It is offering a capability. The DOT system will now give first-come, first-served executions. It will give more certain, speedier execution, similar to what we call Direct+ today. That is all that is changing. We are not having two parallel markets functioning. I do not see that kind of event. Again, orders will go to the best price. Whether it will be the New York Stock Exchange or a competing stock exchange, orders will go to where the best price is. It is that simple.

SCHWARTZ: I would like to get back to your observation, Brett, about intra-minute, intra-second volatility. That certainly does not fit in with what we talk about in our academic studies on the informational efficiency of prices. I would like clarification on two things. First, are you suggesting that it is happening a lot more frequently than the COCO example? Second, on what size trades, big trades or little trades is this happening?

REDFEARN: One of the things I have examined very closely is the process in which official closing prices are determined on the NASDAQ marketplace. At the close, certain market participants are incentivized to move the price in one direction or another, if, for example, they have promised a customer a guaranteed closing price. When we tried to figure out what was a good standard against which to measure a true closing price, we realized that we could not look solely at the actual official closing print, which could be quite random. We could not even look at the last five minutes of trading. We had to look at volume weighted prices over the last 10, 20, 30 seconds, even up to a minute, because the prices at the very end of the day were all over the map. When we started looking at where the volatility was, we saw that, in the last second of trading, there were numerous examples of prints hitting the tape 30 to 35 cents apart, in the same stock, in the same second.

At first we thought this was an aberration. Then we realized that you would see this behavior quite frequently in different types of stocks. With respect to trade size, we observed a lot of small trades, printing all over the map.

ANDRESEN: I thank our panel, George, Chris, Rich, Michael and Brett.

CHAPTER 6: HYBRID MARKETS

Moderator– Mary McDermott-Holland, Franklin Portfolio Associates
Senior Vice President
Michael Buek, The Vanguard Group
Principal
Matthew Celebuski, JP Morgan Securities Inc.
Managing Director
Alfred Eskandar, Liquidnet, Inc.
Director of Marketing
Adena Friedman, The NASDAQ Stock Market
Executive Vice President of Corporate Strategy and Data Products
Robert Gasser
CEO, NYFIX Millennium, President
NYFIX Transaction Service
President, NYFIX Clearing Corporation
Christopher Heckman, Investment Technology Group, Inc.
Managing Director

MARY McDERMOTT-HOLLAND: I am honored that a lot of people I consider my friends and colleagues are here on this panel today. One week ago I sat for eight mind-numbing hours at the SEC open hearings. We heard a lot of themes expressed. Chairman Donaldson was saying how he wanted the participants to take off their firms' hats, and to put on their public policy hats instead. Today, I have asked the panel to do just the opposite: take off their public policy hats, and put on their firm hats. I have asked each panelist to give us a really good perspective about our markets and where we are going from here. Indeed, we have talked a lot today about the past. Now we are going to talk about today as well as the future. In the process, we will focus on some of the themes brought up in the earlier panels.

I have taken a few notes on the pervasive themes at the earlier sessions today. One is connectivity and linkage. It seems to me that, in a fully connected and linked world, the need for a lot of the trade-through rules and de minimus exemptions is non-existent. Let us start by asking our panelists to give us their perspectives on the concept of fast versus slow. And I want to hear their thoughts on the need for the trade-through. Please give us the perspective from your firms on where you see that particular part of Reg NMS going. Chris, how about starting with you?

CHRISTOPHER HECKMAN: Thanks, Mary. If I put on my ITG hat as a broker, it is all about creating efficient technologies for our institutional clients. What that means for us is that we have to build all of these linkages. We have to put in place all of this connectivity so that our clients can reach all of the market centers that they want to reach.

If you look at the market structure of three or four years ago, you will see that back then the over-the-counter market was clearly in a state of flux. We went through a torturous couple of years, building connectivity and technology. We linked our clients to the ECNs. Each of the ECNs at that time had different order types. They all had different levels of reliability and turnaround. Those things were a complicated task that we, along with a lot of other brokers and technology providers, eventually solved. The problem had been that the market structure was fragmented. The brokers stepped in and solved the problem. We did not need the regulators to do that.

Now, in 2004, we are faced with analyzing the quality of the New York Stock Exchange. It is quite clear from my clients that, for liquid stocks, more automation – as in the NASDAQ model – and completely automated interaction, are winning the day. There is no doubt that trading Microsoft is infinitely easier than trading GE. You just cannot argue with that. Whether you look at speed, transparency, depth, or any other measure, our clients tell us that NASDAQ's model is better than the NYSE's.

There is still debate and division when you get into the small-cap and mid-cap arena. In this case, the exchange model still has some value. At ITG, we have algorithmic servers and one of our servers – these servers are all over the street now – attempts to capture VWAP. It seeks to trade an order and mirror the volume weighted average prices. We found, in small-cap names, that we actually do better in the listed market than we do in the over-the-counter market. This shocks our PhD at ITG who actually built the strategy because, in the over-the-counter market, he has transparency. He has all kinds of sophisticated order types. He has depth of book, and he has many more things to draw signals off of. Yet, on some of these smaller-cap names (and this is a fairly large universe of stocks), there are about 600 million shares that we analyzed. For these stocks, he actually does slightly better in the listed world. So, in terms of comparing the New York Stock Exchange to a completely electronic marketplace in the small and mid-cap names, I would say the jury is still out on what the best mechanism is.

McDERMOTT-HOLLAND: Maybe we can take this a step further and talk a bit about the trade-through rule. Adena Friedman, I know that you have some thoughts about it. And Bob Gasser, how about telling us a bit about what is going on with that in your world?

ROBERT GASSER: Ladies first.

ADENA FRIEDMAN: NASDAQ has paid keen attention to what is happening with Reg NMS. In my opinion, there are two provisions within Reg NMS that will have a meaningful, measurable effect on the industry. People here should be paying close attention to them. One is the trade-through rule, and the other is the access provision.

The access provisions have not gotten a lot of airtime. Nevertheless, they will go just as far in creating a fair and linked environment as the trade-through rule. The SEC talks about you having to provide equal access to every participant; that participants will be reaching their markets through broker dealers and not through a planned linkage, which is very efficient.[27] They talk about the fact that they want to bring access fees down to eliminate the fee arbitrage that currently exists in some of the marketplaces. The access provisions are there to create a linked environment using private broker-based or market based-linkages, without having to rely on an antiquated ITS plan, or any other antiquated means. If you take that and all the things that they want to try to do with access, and add on the trade-through rule, then you have to start looking at fast versus slow. You have to provide equal access to any participant who comes in and, with the trade-through rule, every participant must be able to access anyone who is out there with the best price.

We can have a very efficient model, except that we must make sure that a trade-through rule addresses the kind of markets that should be linked. And fast must mean fast. It cannot just mean fast for a hundred shares and

---

[27] In the end, (as noted in Footnote 1, Chapter 4), the Securities and Exchange Commission in Reg NMS did require a 'uniform market access rule that would promote non-discriminatory access to quotations displayed by SRO trading centers through a private linkage approach.'

slow for everything else. It has to mean fast for your full book. And fast means auto execution. When you talk about the fairness of the markets and about how easy it is to trade Microsoft (frankly, I would argue down through the mid-caps), you would find that we do not have a trade-through rule and yet we have a better environment to trade within. But if you are going to have a trade-through rule, fast must mean fast.

ROBERT GASSER: I want to add that, to me, as a trader, trading Microsoft versus GE or the equivalent large super liquid stock, there is absolutely no question that electronically is the more efficient, less costly way to trade. It is more efficient in terms of my time, and I give up less information about who is doing the trading. There is no question. I would love to challenge the New York Stock Exchange to sit down on the trading desk and first try to trade a GE, and then try to trade a Microsoft. It is quite different. I am not sure about the medium and small-cap stocks, however. With them, the jury is still out.

I was very interested to hear that small-cap algorithmic trading was better on the listed side. It probably has to do with the specialist committing capital on small to medium-sized trades. In NASDAQ, no one is responsible for ensuring efficient trading of the stock and for controlling volatility. But for the large liquid stocks, there is no question – electronically is the more efficient way to trade.

FRIEDMAN: One of the things you have to consider is, what are the economics of a specialist? How will the specialists support the smaller stocks, if you are creating a fair, competitive game for the large-cap stocks? For the specialists, the economics are going to change dramatically. Will they be capable of committing that capital on the small-cap names? You must look at the fact that, if you change the way that they trade, you are doing so across all of the stocks. I also want to add that small cap for NASDAQ is different from small cap for New York. When we looked down the Russell 1000, which includes what New York would deem to be small-cap and a lot of mid-cap stocks, we still far exceed New York in terms of effective spreads, speed of execution and liquidity available.

McDERMOTT-HOLLAND: You raise an interesting point about the role of the specialist. I will ask you, Michael, how do you see the specialist's role changing with all of these new proposed regulations? Or should it change?

MICHAEL BUEK: We trade a lot electronically and I am probably biased. We do a lot of basket trading, a lot of electronic trading. When I post a bid in New York, I am out there with 10,000 shares sitting on the bid at $20. If somebody in the crowd is also a buyer and the market tanks for some reason, I bought the stock at 20 and now it is lower. If the market is fairly stable and a 1,000 share market order comes in to hit my bid, the floor presence has an advantage over my electronic presence. The floor presence can say, 'Okay, I will price improve by a penny and step in front.' But, on the other side, when I take liquidity electronically, if I go to take a posted limit offer of ten, for example, and moments later there is a market order buyer in the crowd, the limit offer should be mine. I am the one who made the first move to take this posted limit offer. The buyer in the crowd is hoping that it comes in and, as it turns out, there is an auction. Maybe I split the print or miss the print altogether.

The new environment should protect limit orders. If I do post a limit and someone comes to hit the bid, I am done. The same thing when I act to take an offer. Meanwhile, I would like the specialists to be there committing capital when needed, not just taking advantage of their privileged position.

McDERMOTT-HOLLAND: I heard someone on one of the previous panels say that the buy-side is agnostic as to where we trade, and that New York is the place of last resort. I think that Robert Shapiro mentioned that New York is the place of last resort to get a trade done. Alfred, maybe you can talk a bit about what you are doing for the buy-side in terms of circumventing some of that. You guys at Liquidnet are pulling some of the liquidity away from New York.

ALFRED ESKANDAR: I do not think that we are pulling liquidity away. I do not want to get into the fragmentation argument, but...

McDERMOTT-HOLLAND: We are going to get to fragmentation in a few minutes.

ESKANDAR: It ultimately comes down to looking at the market in a very simple way. At the end of the day, you have a large buyer wanting to meet a large seller. The specialist system right now does not efficiently respond to the needs of the customer. However, the specialists in their current form will change and respond to these needs. If you look at the large caps like the GEs, there is a pretty efficient market. I do not think that you need human intervention with the GEs. You could raise a better argument for the small- and mid-cap stocks. The NASDAQ model has proven that liquid stocks do not need human intervention. I think it is fair to say (talk to any of the buy-side guys in this room) that nobody is really a big fan of price improvement. I am not looking for it, so please do not offer it to me, or try to jam it down my throat. What people are looking for is an efficient way to get their merchandise.

Efficiency to me means getting rid of as many intermediaries as possible and allowing the natural counterparties to interact directly with each other. Whether it is my model or a different model, ultimately that is where the buy-side is going to go anyway. The buy-side is agnostic. They do not necessarily care where they get it done. And that is good. They shouldn't care because, quite frankly, they are not working to make my life better. They are working to make their shareholders wealthier. Whether they execute on Liquidnet, or ITG, or Millennium, or elsewhere, the venue that offers them the greatest value, and that protects them, is the one that is ultimately going to do well.

McDERMOTT-HOLLAND: Competition is driving a lot of this, and we are looking for alternative sources of liquidity. In the search for liquidity, which is what the buy-side ultimately wants, there is a lot of competition. Adena, we talked a bit about the closing cross and the competition. There has been a lot of controversy surrounding closing prices on NASDAQ. The Amex received approval for a pilot of several stocks from S&P, and the competitive pressure forced NASDAQ's hand. It forced you guys to develop your closing cross, which is in the midst of a full rollout as we speak. Maybe you can talk a bit about competition, and how it is driving your closing cross product.

FRIEDMAN: Competition is always better than a regulatory solution. To the extent that the SEC is trying to create a fair and equal competitive environment, we support its efforts in Reg NMS. But, in general, competition is what drives us to innovate. NASDAQ did innovate this spring. We created a closing cross. We had been looking to do that for a long time. But I would certainly say that the timeline for creating the closing cross was pushed up with the announcement that S&P was looking at Amex to close the market in 12 stocks. That was an eye-opener. So we embarked on a very aggressive campaign to work with the industry, and to work with our own technology folks to create a closing cross that truly meets investors' needs. We launched it in April, 2004, and we are in rollout mode right now. We have 80 stocks rolled into it and it has been very successful. It is working well. It may be too early to tell, it is only three and a half weeks in now, but we are very pleased with how it is going.[28]

---

[28] Share volume in NASDAQ's closing cross hovered around 0.50% in the first half of 2005, according to NASDAQ data. However, there was a notable one day

McDERMOTT-HOLLAND: We have danced around this trade-through topic today. But we have not focused much on the opt-out proposal in Reg NMS,[29] which seems to be one of the most contentious pieces, at least from the buy-side perspective. Does anybody want to give us their perspective on opt-out? I know, Michael, that you have a definite opinion about it.

BUEK: As far as the trade-through rule goes, the intent behind it is the retail investor, the smaller investor. People in this room are not trading a thousand shares. They are trading two million shares. The trade-through rule has no impact there.

Michael LaBranche said earlier that he would like to have caveat emptor, let the buyer beware and let the market shake it out. There is a problem with that. The problem is that the market does not have the information. If you do not know that you have been wronged, there is no way to address the wrong. In that short time frame when that trade is on the floor, and it is sitting with Michael, and it is sitting with the floor brokers in front of him, you do not have access to that information. You do not have access to information about what the floor brokers are doing, what they are trading, or about what else is trading. So, from a retail standpoint, trade-through probably is a good thing. But operationally, it will be very difficult. Time frames will have to be worked out, and the de minimus spread specified.

---

spike for the Quad Witch on March 18, 2005, when the cross accounted for 4.64 percent of NASDAQ share volume, or 104,622,118 shares; and there was another notable one day spike for the Quad Witch on June 17, 2005, when the closing cross accounted for 2.21 percent of NASDAQ share volume, or 52,343,000 shares. Separately, a study by brokerage firm White Cap Trading contended that NASDAQ's electronic closing cross performed better than the New York Stock Exchange's manual cross at the close. For further analysis, see Michael Pagano and Robert A. Schwartz, 'NASDAQ's Closing Cross: Has its new call auction given NASDAQ better closing prices? Early Findings,' Journal of Portfolio Management, Summer 2005, pages 100-111.

[29] In Reg NMS, adapted by a divided SEC on April 6, 2005 (as noted in a separate chapter), protections in the trade-through rule – which had operated on the NYSE – were toughened and extended to NASDAQ. The rule curbs a broker – with some exceptions – from executing a trade at a price inferior to another price that would have been available. The general 'opt-out' exceptions once envisaged for Reg NMS were not adapted. The SEC only made exceptions in Reg NMS for intermarket sweeps, flickering quotations and prices that are not immediately and electronically accessible.

That brings us to the people in this room. Many of you here are going to want to use the opt-out rule for one reason or another. You are not looking for the thousand- share liquidity. You are looking for the 50,000-share, the 100,000-share liquidity. For you, having to show that, or having to hit 20 markets in order to get the business done, probably will not help. Where it does help us is with algorithmic trading.

Also, the hybrid market on the NYSE helps us with algorithmic trading. It helps us because we trade at a known price and a known size, and the report comes back very quickly. We have seen progress in this area. This is partly a function of our brokers now vetting the overall market through smart routers before the trade ever gets to the floor. ITG and ArcaEx are examples of brokers offering smart routing. But we have found that more of the liquidity is going down to the floor in algorithmic trading. You have these short-term handshakes of a thousand shares. In the game theory example used this morning in the Nash equilibrium, if both criminals tell on each other (by the way, I was uncomfortable with them being criminals) they both get bad outcomes. If you have ten million shares and you show your hand, you get a bad outcome. But if you show your hand a thousand shares at a time for a thousand trades, then you are shaking hands and you are meeting that buyer or seller continually throughout the day. We are seeing less and less block flow, and we are seeing more and more algorithmic flow.

UNIDENTIFIED SPEAKER: Then there is the poor guy who shows up with a block to trade in the traditional way. Say 100 shares, 200 shares, or 300 shares. He waits for the other side, but the other side has decided to go electronic. So it gets tougher and tougher for the big blocks to meet when more people adapt the algorithmic trading strategies.

BUEK: Right. That is really fragmenting liquidity. The specialist still has a role. He can search the immediate market for an order or for liquidity, and it could be in the crowd. But the smaller orders are continually going to go electronic. If the crowd wants to join in at some point, they will join in. I believe that the floor brokers can actually hit the electronic market from their handhelds so that you can still participate in that liquidity.

CELEBUSKI: To weigh in on the opt-out provision, I say that it is an unfortunate outcome of something that is turning into a religious debate amongst market participants. It is almost like Bush vs. Kerry. Opinion seems to be evenly divided, with a very small number of undecideds.

What we learned this morning from Rob Shapiro, Paul Davis and now from Mike Buek as well, is that the institutions are today the great free market force. They are voting with their feet. They are much more willing to scrape a Liquidnet, or scrape a Millennium, before they expose an order to the floor. What does that tell us? It tells us that there is a profound lack of trust in intermediaries today. The intermediaries can have a big effect in terms of slippage, market impact, and all the things that Wayne Wagner has been studying for years.

But, at the end of the day, it presents us with a national market system and a great opportunity to address the real issue – linkages and competition. I have only heard one speaker today talk about ITS and the role it could possibly play in linking the marketplaces. I have not heard one speaker talk about the role of liability and how it has played a role in changing the NASDAQ marketplace.

I have heard officials from the New York Stock Exchange (it is actually a great breath of fresh air) admit to trading through, admit to the fact that, yeah, it happens. There are good, there are mediocre, and there are bad specialists out there. It is just a fact of life. But there are guys out there who are trying to get to that quote, and they cannot do so because they do not have the technology. It is not only about bad specialist behavior. It is about the encumbrances of operating within the New York Stock Exchange today. Liability would change all of that. With liability, we would not have to do a thing if Arca was traded through. There would be no appeal process. It is done; it is time stamped, right down to the millisecond. All of the technology exists today to make that happen.

The religious debate has gotten a little out of hand. It was focused on the three amigos: Reg NMS, opt-out provisions, and the fast market-slow market distinction. I say, let the customer decide. For the first time in our professional lifetimes (at least in my professional lifetime), the buy-side is taking an aggressive stance. That is worth waiting for.

FRIEDMAN: So are you advocating not having a rule? Should we just let competition define...

CELEBUSKI: I say let the trade-through rule stand and let it be properly enforced. If it is enforced, there is liability. If something needs to be arbitrated, let the SEC arbitrate. I am not advocating an industry-wide SRO. That, for a lot of people, would be absolute heresy. But if something needs to be adjudicated between say, NASDAQ, Boston, the Midwest and Arca, and between all the other pieces of the national market system and the New York Stock Exchange, fine. Maybe it is a real ITS that is required, maybe it is real linkage, maybe it is a real cooperative, not one that is jaundiced from the standpoint of the current governance that it enjoys.

BUEK: But you do have issues when you go to multiple levels of the New York book; you have someone trying to hit orders electronically and walk a book up. But New York is saying that we want people to have the choice of going to the auction market. So you are not able to just ping New York up ten cents. For the first level, yes. But then they have decided to basically opt out the rest of their book from autoex because there is an auction.

CELEBUSKI: That is fine. They should have every right to do that.

BUEK: So, if there was a New York offer at 5 in the new environment where they are fast, and a New York offer at 6, say 500 shares both times, Arca will offer at ten cents. You want to get that Arca offer as fast as possible. Of course, as a trader, I would love to take New York at five, take New York at six, and then take Arca in half a second. But if I can only take New York at five and then go through the auction process for the six cents, I will have to trade-through it. I do not want to. I want to take the six cents, but doing so will slow me down and start an auction. If I then have to wait 12 or 15 seconds, I simply have to trade-through it.

ESKANDAR: What you have just articulated, Mike, is one of the main themes that was brought out today. One of the big questions that we all will hopefully walk away with is whether or not price improvement, as defined by the New York Stock Exchange, is a necessity. Is there the potential to create (I am not going to talk about the clock because that would head us off in another direction) a linked marketplace that is smart enough to aggregate quotes at price points and, in effect, to create liquidity, posted liquidity? Think about the New York Stock Exchange today. It is a bit counterintuitive in that they charge people to post. That is diametrically opposed to the ECN marketplace.

Island and Matt Andresen created an industry around paying people to provide liquidity. We can, of course, argue about whether or not those were good guys or bad guys but, either way, they were posting liquidity. Perhaps New York kicks in some market data fees for doing that. Nevertheless, at the end of the day, there is no mechanism in place. We have not talked about things that will improve liquidity taking in the listed world. That is part and parcel of what I am talking about. If you have a linked market with people feeling confident that there will be autoex and auto quote, you will see a tremendous surge...

BUEK: The limit order book would be fuller than it is now.

FRIEDMAN: When you say do not let the SEC regulate it, just let competition decide how it is going to go, I can tell you, as the senior negotiator on the UTP Plan[30] for NASDAQ, that it is a broken system. You are talking about trying to make a fundamental change to ITS where...

BUEK: COCO – Corinthian Colleges – proved that last December when trading was temporarily halted in this NASDAQ stock, reportedly because of a system problem.

FRIEDMAN: A bunch of different markets have to come together. We are all incredible competitors, and we agree on some things. ITS is probably the most broken of all the plans. I say let competition reign. Let Lava and ITG and all of these other competitors come and build those linkages. We do not need an industry utility linkage anymore. The technology has gone well past that. If you want to put liability on an exchange that trades through another exchange, that is a different mechanism. You do not need plan linkage for that.[31] You were talking about DTCC[32] or some super regulator. In the end, I say do away with the trade-through rule and let competition really reign. That is the environment that NASDAQ operates in. We have looked deeply at whether we trade-through more or less than New York. We found that we trade-through less in NASDAQ because the linkage is efficient and best execution reigns. Best execution is more complex than just looking at the best price. It is looking for speed, it is looking for fill rates, it is looking for market impact and price. Let all of these factors determine how the linkages are built. Give the customer control over where the orders go and let competition work. Let us not have this antiquated trade-through rule that still keeps some competitive power in the hands of the specialists.

---

[30] Unlisted Trading Privileges Plan.

[31] The Linkage Plan – called the Intermarket Trading System, or ITS – is used in the trading of NYSE and Amex listed stocks in nine markets which include the NYSE, Archipelago Exchange, the CBOE and NASDAQ. NASD members participate in ITS through a facility of the NASDAQ market, known as the Computer Assisted Executed System, or CAES. Under the terms of the Linkage Plan plan, SROs are required to contract with each other for access with unexecuted, or 'open' orders, from one SRO to another. Some analysts say the ITS would become irrelevant under the parameters of Reg NMS. In that case, ITS was expected to be replaced by a model in which private companies, as well as the exchanges themselves, provide linkages across exchanges. Nevertheless, an early assessment of Reg NMS by one NYSE official was that ITS would continue to operate in conjunction with the 'fast rules' of Reg NMS.

[32] Depository Trust & Clearing Corporation.

HECKMAN: I would add one more thing to Adena's comment. If you are defining best execution, you must understand that there are multiple participants in the market who have multiple needs. You cannot forget about size. It boggles my mind. I was sitting at the SEC hearings that you were at as well, and it was always an argument of speed versus best price. That is great, but what do I care if I get 200 shares at the best price in a split nanosecond? I have three million more to finish. How does that help me, how does that help my shareholders?

There has been a lack of discussion about the different participants in the marketplace, and about how they each need to be serviced. Quite frankly, I am not sure how you can serve two masters with one market.

Obviously, I am a bit self-serving in my statements here. But it is something that we recognize because you cannot expect institutions to display their full size. I do not care what kind of book it is. No institution is going to put up their full interest on a central limit order book. Look at the European exchanges. They are all electronic, but look at the depth of their books.

When talking about market structure, it is important to understand that there are institutional investors, and that there are retail investors. Retail investors who directly own equity shares, believe it or not, are about 23 million strong in the U.S. But there are 94 million plus who own mutual funds. So the legislation that is coming in will benefit one out of three people in the market. That really needs to be brought to the forefront.

BUEK: That small 200-share limit order may be all that I have. Maybe it is the life savings of somebody, 200 shares at 05. If that person is posted in a fast market, it does not cost him anything to go there. In fact, as a buyer, I want to take that. If I am going to cross 100,000 on Liquidnet up ten cents, I want to take the guy at 05 first. That is, if it does not cost me any time. But, if I have to go through the auction process and wait 30 seconds or so, I am going to trade-through the little guy. But I do not think that that limit order should be traded through.

HECKMAN: I am not saying that it should be. In fact, 96 percent of my executions are within the spread. But I have to worry about the four percent that are outside of the spread.

BUEK: Say I want to reach for the name. Just make me route out, or have your system automatically route out. If it is electronic and accessible, take it. Then print up because maybe next time I am posting out there for a thousand shares and I will get it done.

ESKANDAR: You are saying that the trade-through rule should apply to all of the exchanges and to the depth for all their books, that you should hit this book, the next book, the next book, and so on.

BUEK: If they are autoex, and there is no time to take it, as someone who is taking liquidity, that is what I want to do. Certainly as someone who is posting liquidity, I want to be taken out before something trades above me. If it is a slow market, then it is a different story.

CELEBUSKI: The only way that the Exchange can play in that game, is if the quote is a liability quote, right?[33] Isn't that the crux of it, isn't that one of the bigger issues here?

McDERMOTT-HOLLAND: I would be interested in hearing what other people in the audience think.

ALLAN GRODY (Financial Intergroup) [From the Floor]: This is a dilemma that we have had for 40 years ever since price and time were put up as the definitive way of integrating markets. And it resulted in a CLOB proposal – based on price/time priority -that is everything in one big black box. Back then it was recognized that you could not have time priority across distributed market centers. Well, guess what? We have taken this argument up to the trade-through rule, and the dilemma is that the technology, as good as it is, is not going to enable you to have no trade-through rule. That's because with advanced technology it becomes easier to trade-through prices.

For example, you will send orders to the best quoted markets because you will be doing 25 quotes a second times ten. The guy who, earlier in the game, figures out how to do it faster is going to get all the order flow and everyone else is going to sit there. So we have a dilemma between the concept and the technology. You have heard a few people talk about that. When you get right down to it, practical implementation considerations won't allow us to reach out to the best quoted markets at any point in time, unless we go back to the old sore about the clock sequencing the trades and put them into one central machine. Then we do not have a problem. But we do not want to put them into one central machine because then we deconstruct the competitive marketplace, a marketplace that has given us all these great reasons to have these seminars (laughter).

McDERMOTT-HOLLAND: It is frightening that we can all be away from work so much. Anybody want to take that?

---

[33] A liability quote is essentially the same as a 'firm quote,' which is a quote that requires the quoting party to trade if presented with an order.

CELEBUSKI: I will take it. That technology might not be there to the millisecond, but we use a system, other people use systems, and we think we can provide that now. In fact, we are held to providing that for our clients as a part of the best execution that we deliver. We have to look for the best market to execute in. Whatever is on our machine at that time would be the best market to execute in. Will the order be there when we send in the trade? We do not know, but it is worth sending the trade there for exactly that reason.

FRIEDMAN: The markets that compete in the NASDAQ environment in general have about a ten millisecond turnaround time. The reason for that is that we have to compete for order flow. We do not have a trade-through rule. Not having one is driving the competition. It is not a situation where one market is winning all of the order flow. It truly is a competitive environment.

Even within the New York space, you have 22 percent of the market share. Elsewhere, if you have a trade-through rule and you have five different markets that have to link up (and let us say that you have a very narrowly defined trade-through rule), then if you want to get 10,000 shares done, and you send 2,000 to the first market, and 2,000 to the second market, and 2,000 to the third market, etc., you disperse the order across all five markets. If you send it simultaneously to get all five done, the second market is going to reject it because the first market has not quite gotten it, and if it is simultaneously sent, the third market will also reject it and send it to the second market, etc., etc. That is an impossible situation. So you are right. Unless it is a CLOB, you will have a really hard time implementing a preventative trade-through rule that is strict, and that has no ability for the customer to opt out.

CRAIG ROTHFELD (W.J. Bonfanti) [From the Floor]: In keeping with the theme of hybrid markets, I have a question for the panel about algorithmic trading. Michael Buek made the point earlier that if you have a million shares to buy and you are not able to find the liquidity, then maybe you dice it up into a thousand trades of a thousand shares each. We all know that about 45 percent of the business is going to the New York whether it be program trading or algorithmic trading. Is there a feeling amongst yourselves that algorithmic and program trading is just the way it is going to go, and that those percentages will go higher and higher? Or, is there something in the current debate about market reforms that would actually include rolling that back to a point where it would be less about getting size done on an algorithmic basis? Would you be able to go back to getting blocks done for 10,000 shares or more – instead of today's typical trade size of several hundred shares – and have price discovery for size?

UNIDENTIFIED SPEAKER: I have a view on the algorithmic trading products. What it comes down to is anonymity. It is another tool for buy-side traders to take control of their order flow, to maintain their equilibrium with the volume that is traded during the course of the day. But it still gives them the option to cancel that order in a millisecond and to respond to liquidity whether or not it is inbound from the floor, or it is inbound from a broker dealer, or it is inbound from Liquidnet or Millennium, etc., etc.

At the end of the day, algorithms have become the great beard in the marketplace. It used to be a Midwest broker who you gave that order to. Now it is an algorithm. It is reflective not only of the change in buy-side trading behavior and capability. It is also a trend that is symptomatic of a profound lack of trust in some circumstances.

HECKMAN: Mary, if I could. I think we all have Wayne Wagner to blame for this. If it was not for Wayne and Plexus and the other trading cost vendors, a lot of this stuff would not be here. Quite frankly, the buy-side would not care as much. When you have people watching costs, you have people looking at performance, and there is competition for investor dollars going to the funds that give you the best returns year after year. Guess what? The buy-side firms now want to take more control of their order flow. Buy-side firms are actually executing more of their own order flow each day. As a percentage of total order flow, you guys are going to do more and more yourself. This is not just from the Liquidnets of the world. It is the actual sell-side broker dealers as well. They are giving you algorithmic tools, and they are putting them on your desktop. You have access to Lava and the other aggregators. Soon you guys will be almost self-sufficient in a sense.

FRIEDMAN: Another reason the buy-side is taking control is that you have been given tools to take control. I have been doing this for almost 25 years, and I can tell you that 25 years ago we were writing things down on pieces of paper and flipping them. We needed intermediaries back then. Technology and the advent of an order management system have allowed us to take control of that order flow. Yes, Wayne has made us focus a lot on trading costs, and technology has empowered us.

HECKMAN: We are a transaction cost vendor. We are not an advocate of slicing and dicing, or of using VWAP as the appropriate benchmark for most institutional trading. But, at the end of the day, we are about providing our clients with what they want. For a decent majority of our clients, VWAP seems to be the appropriate benchmark. Would I love to go back to the days when every order was submitted in its entirety into the first POSIT of the day? Absolutely. But it is a different world today. That is why we run 13 crosses instead of one. People have really changed the way they implement trading.

McDERMOTT-HOLLAND: I am going to let Wayne answer this because he was put on the spot here.

WAYNE WAGNER (Plexus Group) [From the Floor]: There is a third reason why buy-side traders are taking more control (we should really ask this of the buy-side traders). The third reason is that, to some degree, they have lost control of their brokers. They have lost control with the rise of more prying eyes, and hedge funds, and day traders, and people who are reading the signals within the market rather than reading signals from the economy outside of the market.

BUEK: I feel like we have been more empowered by the tools that have been given to us than by the paranoia of people shopping our orders around. Before '97, you could not even drive the quote in NASDAQ as a buy-sider. Back then, you had to force the broker to show it. That has really changed. Seven to ten years ago, the buy-side trader was thought of as an administrator. The PM would give you the list and you just decided which broker to pay. Then, when the brokers' executions came back, you gave them a hard time for doing a poor job. But you did not actually trade the shares yourself. Now, with the advent of the ECNs, and POSIT, and Liquidnet, we have been empowered. For that matter, so has the individual investor.

Back in the old days, when NASDAQ was 50-cent wide and Instinet was a teeny-wide, the individual investor was having a tough time. Now they can drive a quote as well. And buy-side traders are thought of more as professionals. We are analyzing our costs. We know that there is a lot of leakage. We are analyzing how we route and control the order. I think that it is not out of fear of leakage, but because we have the tools. It is because more buy-siders are taking control. Pre-'97, you could call a market maker and he or she would know where the bodies were buried. A market maker would know that there were three buyers at these limits, and a couple of sellers at those limits. Now those guys are trading themselves. So you go to the market maker for some capital or perhaps the electronic system is trading 90 percent of your stock. So you may decide to take control of your order yourself.

Just one point about VWAP. I do not know if VWAP is a real benchmark. It is more that you are giving up because, typically, when a portfolio manager gives me an order, he wants it done right now, and you ask yourself the following question: 'Am I going to have impact and get it done quickly and ask for some capital, or am I going to spread it out throughout the day and incur opportunity costs?' The algorithms are one step better than VWAP. For example, if I have 100,000 shares of Cisco, I had better not spread that out over the whole day. I can get Cisco done right now. But a smaller cap, like Stanley Works,[34] could be spread out over the day. Hopefully, I can find the other side in Liquidnet or POSIT. On the other hand, if a broker calls me on this stock, I can stop my algorithmic trading and find the natural, which is really what we are looking for. We want to find the natural without opening up. The worst thing that you can do is open up. I am here with a million, and I find out that nobody is there because you have given that up. And then you have nothing to show for it.

ESKANDAR: Ten years ago, you would have called a broker. He would have bought it a point down. Bob Wood showed me some stuff yesterday that he has been working on, some preliminary results about looking at stationarity in the markets.[35] It seems that, over the last ten years, markets have become much less stationary. Back then, you had markets with increments of a quarter or 50 cents. The equilibrium price was somewhere in there. Then prices would jump, and then it would stay at that jump point when a block trade hit.

McDERMOTT-HOLLAND: It must make you proud, Wayne, to be the father of opportunity costs. I have a question. Can the hybrid auction market and the electronic market co-exist peacefully? Can this work? Is there a way that this concept can succeed?

HECKMAN: I personally believe that there is a way. Over time, humans have added quite a bit to market openings and to market closings. The Google experience with a Dutch auction is an interesting example. But there is quite a bit of discretion that will be exercised around a clearing print and a clearing price. The reason for that is that you do not want a market to get into a state of mania. All markets have the potential to do that and, for that reason, I think that there is a role for a human to play.

---

[34] (NYSE:SWK).

[35] Sugato Chakravarty, Frederick H. deB. Harris and Robert A. Wood, 'The Changing State of the Markets: Common Factors and Impulse Responses for Cointegrated Spreads and Depths,' working paper, University of Memphis.

And there is the routine stuff. The vast majority of people would agree that, in the top 100 stocks in terms of market cap and liquidity, and during the course of a routine trading day, there is not much value added by a human. We could argue that point as you go down the spectrum of stocks in terms of their liquidity to mid- and small-cap. But at the end of the day, there is a role for a human.

Mike LaBranche mentioned the CME earlier on. The CME is a great example of an exchange that de-mutual zed, created competing marketplaces within its own products, and has slowly migrated towards the human where it makes the most sense, and towards a fully-electronic marketplace where that makes the most sense. There is clearly a role for a human to play, whether as an intermediary, a block trader, or a market maker. But it is only the extreme cases where supply and demand needs to be matched up. The counterparties need to walk away having received a significant amount of liquidity and feeling good about that clearing price. There are hundreds of data points that go into the determination that that was the right size in Stanley Works for the eight guys who participated in that block.

McDERMOTT-HOLLAND: Michael, that was your question. Do you want to expand upon it?

BUEK: There are definitely advantages with a human intermediary at the open and the close, where imbalances come up and errors need to be corrected. But the advantage that the floor presence has over electronic orders, or limit orders that are just sitting on the book, is an inequity that we can clear up. The floor and the electronics can co-exist. Maybe in some instance, say a stock is offered at .05 for 5,000 shares, and someone decides to take that via regular DOT, not Direct+, so you are exposing it to the auction process. Maybe you are going to get price improvement. You are taking a chance that there will be a delay. You accept that risk. So you are out 5,000 to pay .05, and three seconds later I send a Direct+ order in to take it. It is still displayed. I do not know if that can co-exist but, in my mind, if it is a hybrid, the Direct+ order takes the stock. Or you can imagine two guys in the crowd, and I guess the floor brokers will have handhelds to do Direct+. They are both buyers waiting around for a sell, 5,000 shares are there, and one guy who is sitting next to the other says, 'Hey, who took that? Someone just took that, and I didn't get a chance to participate.' I do not know how that is going to work. It is not as easy as it appears. In theory, it can be great for certain instances. But I am not so sure that the big liquid stocks need it.

FRIEDMAN: In our world, we consider a hybrid market the combination of a continuous market and a call auction when you need to have one. With the closing cross that we now have, we have created an electronic auction at the close of the day, and we are planning to create one at the open.[36] We recognized that the industry needs a continuous market that is highly electronic on an everyday basis. But at the open and at the close, when there is so much capital at stake and liquidity in the market, it is important for people to be able to react to imbalances and to find the proper clearing price. This is not simply relying on supply and demand alone. That is why NASDAQ created the cross, and it is what we will be doing with the open as well.

We believe that a hybrid market does not necessarily have to have a specialist in the middle. The need is to have capital available at critical points in the day. That is where you have the proper functioning of a hybrid market that incorporates the benefits of electronic speed.

UNIDENTIFIED SPEAKER: Maybe you think that the specialist system is better for small- and mid-caps because the specialist will fill in and will not let price gap up. As you are trading those names in NASDAQ, I know that we do not send in 2,000-share market orders. We show limit orders and display small size so that people will not jump in front. We have changed our style of trading. If one of those names happens to be volatile because of the occasional market order that can come into a small NASDAQ name, we can line the market with bids. Consequently, rather than a situation where a stock would just rip down 60 cents, people see it trade back up again. If I am positioned there, prepared with limit orders to capture that volatility, as long as my limit orders are given fair treatment, I can adapt and trade that way.

McDERMOTT-HOLLAND: Go ahead, Bob.

ROBERT WOOD (University of Memphis) [From the Floor]: Extending that point, it is just Economics 101. Think about the shape of the supply and demand curves – they form a V. The vertex of the V is at the spread midpoint. We know that the better the price you give me, the more I am willing to buy or to sell, where a better price is the distance from the

---

[36] NASDAQ's opening cross became fully functional on December, 2004. Share volume hovered around 0.50% of daily NASDAQ share volume in the first half of 2005, according to NASDAQ data. However, like the closing cross, there were notable spikes in volume on the two Quad Witch days reported by NASDAQ: 6.32 percent of NASDAQ volume, or 142,432,052 shares on March 18, 2005; 10.72 percent of NASDAQ volume, or 254,061,795 shares, on June 17, 2005.

vertex, the distance from the midpoint. So looking back, the 1/8th tick size was a huge spread, a huge barrier to price competition as was the 1/16th tick size. Now we have removed those barriers to price competition.

It used to be that you could put a huge quantity on the bid and the ask, and make tons of money from the bid-ask bounce. You cannot do that anymore. Those who want to go back to the days when you had all that liquidity out there, are ignoring the huge advantage that comes from price competition. The buy-side ought to rejoice at decimalization because it is giving you much stronger price competition. But it also means that you have got to do exactly the kind of thing you are talking about.

You do not necessarily put everything right up there, a penny off, right at the BBO. You stagger stuff going up. If you do that, you are capturing those liquidity events that drive you up or down the book. You can benefit if somebody is really aggressive and wants to buy in a big hurry, and if that person is going to drive up the book. You can earn that spread as a patient trader. This is recognition that we have removed this huge barrier to price competition. This is the new world that we are in. You must adjust your strategies accordingly. The Liquidnet idea and the crossing ideas are great in this environment. They are great, that is, if you can collect the liquidity and centralize it. Other than that, if you are a patient trader, you must stagger things up the book exactly as Michael Buek said.

McDERMOTT-HOLLAND: You made an important point. The key is centralizing that liquidity. Right now, if you have various bids and offers out there, they have to be in multiple venues because the markets are not interlinked. That is part of the problem. We have to be in a number of different places at once. We have a number of tools at our disposal and we must use them all. But at some point, you get overwrought with technology if everything is not linked together. Michael, you and the people at Vanguard talk a lot about the value of a limit order, about bringing the limit order back, and about rewarding the limit order. Do you see block trading coming back to this market? Do you envision a time in our future when we will not be breaking our orders up into multiple slices, when we will be willing to go to a central place and put on a block of stock like we used to do?

BUEK: I do not because we do not like to give up anonymity. I will check Liquidnet and hopefully find the other side there. But if I have to go into a market center and start taking liquidity out of that market, I will go in small. Now, in the big NASDAQ names, the liquidity is there. It may be 20,000 different trades, but you can trade. You can do 500,000 of Cisco in an hour and think nothing of it. To me, what is the big deal? You get 500,000 done pretty quickly. You do not waste any time shopping around. There is no chance that there is leakage going on. I am done and I do not spend a lot of time and effort either calling people or negotiating back and forth.

I am fine with the way it is now. I do not need that one big print. In fact, it seems like a lot of the transaction cost analysis people are more afraid of looking bad than of taking a shot at looking good. So there is a tendency, even if you found that block, you are a natural trader, you have a million shares, you found someone who you know only has a million, and that they are not going to bring in anything more. Even in this case, people are afraid to take the trade – maybe there is news out and the stock is going to go down. To me, that is what you are living for but, instead, you are more afraid of looking bad. So maybe you choose VWAP even though VWAP really is not your benchmark.

I do not think that the blocks will come back. You know, the guy who is out there in the crowd with 200,000. I do not think that he will find the 200,000 on the other side.

McDERMOTT-HOLLAND: Interesting. This has all been very interesting. Thank you all very much.

CHAPTER 7: ELECTRONIC AND FLOOR-BASED TRADING: THE NYSE HYBRID MARKET

Catherine Kinney

President & Co-Chief Operating Officer, New York Stock Exchange

LAWRENCE ZICKLIN: This is a propitious time for the securities markets. Having spent 40 years in the industry with Merrill Lynch and Newberger Berman, I am speaking from personal experience. I have become an observer looking at this extraordinary industry from the outside. Indeed, these are times that are parallel to the mid-1970s when we deregulated commissions. We are now at that kind of a turning -point again. There has been a lot of scandal reported in the financial industry, in the trading industry, and at the New York Stock Exchange. In the midst of all that is happening, it is a privilege to listen to Catherine Kinney of the New York Stock Exchange.

Let me give you a minute's worth of background. She has been President and Co-Chief Operating Officer of the New York Stock Exchange since January of 2002. She is also a member of the Office of the Chairman, and she co-chairs the New York Stock Exchange's management and operating committees. Prior to this, Ms. Kinney was group executive vice president, overseeing the exchange's competitive position, relationships with listed companies, member firms, and institutions, as well as the NYSEs new listings in client service, equity marketing, sales, exchange traded funds and fixed income divisions. In short, she has been busy.

Prior to all of this, Catherine Kinney was responsible for managing trading operations and technology. She also worked in several departments of the exchange, including regulation, sales and marketing, and technology planning. It is my pleasure to introduce her. Catherine Kinney, welcome. The microphone is yours.

CATHERINE KINNEY: Thank you. This must be the toughest spot on the program. I am between you and a drink after a long day. I have to say thanks to you, Larry Zicklin and to Bob Schwartz for bringing everyone together today. The last panel was very interesting. I want to use it as a jumping off point for my presentation this evening.

The title of this conference is Electronic vs. Floor Based Trading. It is an intelligent title, but I do not think that we are facing an either/or proposition. It should not be a choice of one or the other. You heard some of the professionals recommend both, if that is possible. I will talk today about how the New York Stock Exchange intends to execute the Exchange's proposed hybrid model. While it is a challenging project, the history of the New York Stock Exchange would suggest that it can be accomplished. Hopefully, it will be successful for the customers who are in this room.

I will get started by recalling what Bill Donaldson said in a speech this past Sunday to the Society of American Business Editors and Writers in Fort Worth. It supports my opinion. Bill said, 'The leadership of our market depends on going to the benefits of technology while maintaining the advantages of the floor auction model for all investors.' I will therefore start with that as my premise. I also wish to note that the SEC is clearly signaling that it thinks the hybrid model can be effective.

I will make three points. First, I want to challenge the proposition of floor-based versus electronic for listed securities. Second, I would like to describe how the exchange will achieve the hybrid model. This certainly is a work in progress, but we have enough of the elements in place to give you a sense of where we are going. I cannot tell you how it warms me to hear our customers talk about a lot of our products. They have a good understanding of those products. Third, I want to discuss the road ahead.

Before I challenge the proposition of electronic versus floor, I would like to review the list of customer needs that we see. First, everybody wants a deep liquidity pool. I believe that most people would favor a centralized market to achieve that deep liquidity. Our customers clearly want speed. Our customers want efficient access to quotes. They want certainty. They want anonymity. They want high levels of transparency, and they want to protect limit orders. They want low-cost executions.

You heard some of the professionals say, and I agree, that with all of the tools that Wayne Wagner and his peers are developing, there will be a more balanced measurement scorecard on execution costs and market impact. Customers want capital, either from the marketplace or from the sell-side. The sell-side obviously has to fulfill its responsibility to achieve best execution. I suggest that the ideal way to respond is the creation of the right market structure and the best technology, to deliver great service at low cost. Before we discuss exactly how the Exchange hopes to achieve this hybrid model, I will examine where we start from at the New York Stock Exchange.

We believe in a centralized model. We have been trying to commingle a model that includes both institutional investors and retail investors. As many people in the room have pointed out, we have overlaid several things onto that – more professional trading, statistical arbitrage, program trading, and all sorts of other customers into the mix. We are trying to commingle all those customers to create that deep liquidity pool.

The market infrastructure at the Exchange has been very successful. What are the elements of that success? You start with quotes and the advertised quotes. The exchange is putting out nine million quotes a day. We are setting the NBBO. We are the best price 93 percent of the time. We have an open limit order book that is refreshed every five seconds.[37] From our perspective, we are setting the market. We are setting the pace. The fact that we are setting the price is an important benchmark relative to the advertisement of what you can do on the floor of the Exchange.

The next important point about the infrastructure that I will call your attention to are the execution services themselves. We are handling about 12 million orders a day in DOT. We provide lots of choices. You can use DOT, you can use a completely automatic execution system called Direct+, and you can use Institutional Express. You can also use anonymous DOT.[38]

You can be sponsored by a broker dealer and come directly into the markets, without the aid or assistance of that broker, for anything other than

---

[37] NYSE OpenBook real-time is currently in testing and awaiting SEC approval.

[38] Anonymous SuperDot® (ADot) enables institutional investors sponsored by a member firm to submit orders directly to the NYSE without the Exchange, member firm, specialist or floor brokers knowing their identity.

clearing arrangements and membership. It is important to point out, with all of that order execution, that you are getting a 10.7-second turnaround time today.[39]

You have heard that there is strong need for the hybrid in the openings and closings. It is true that the New York Stock Exchange has the higher fill rate or certainty of execution. Today seven percent of the orders on the floor of the exchange are market orders; all the rest of them are limit orders. There has been a big transition in terms of the kind of order population that we are processing. For marketable limits, the fill rate is at 79 percent through DOT. It is actually slightly above 80 percent in ITS.

Specialists and brokers who really create value are the third part of the infrastructure in place today. They are the professionals who fit in the middle of the auction. We have the order flow and the limit order book, but we also have the brokers and the specialists. The specialists are one of the capital providers in the marketplace. Their participation rate is about 9.3 percent today.[40] It is the floor brokers and the order flow coming through DOT that largely make up the quotations that set the NBBO today. The specialists overlay their capital when necessary. This is a very important point. The brokers are representing their customers' interests in ways that are appropriate between that customer and that broker. The floor brokers are also very valuable in the construction of the auction market model.

We start with a very important, valid, and successful infrastructure. What do we produce as a consequence of that infrastructure? What is the quality of our market today? It is important to make three points about market quality. First, we have the lowest effective spreads for the top 200 stocks. Despite what you have heard on many of these panels, call up the SEC Website and look at a 2001 paper that has recreated the SEC's own study from 2000.[41] You will see, for the top 200 stocks, that the effective spreads for the New York Stock Exchange are 71 percent lower than they are for the top 200 NASDAQ stocks.

The second point is our lower volatility. I said earlier that we are trying to balance investor interests, both large and small. What is also important is that we are trying to balance the interest of issuers who have listed their shares on the New York Stock Exchange. The listed companies

---

[39] The 10.7 second turnaround time was as of the first quarter of 2005.

[40] The 9.3 percent participation rate was as of the first quarter of 2005.

[41] Office of Economic Analysis: Report on the Comparison of Order Executions Across Equity Market Structures, Executive Summary, January 8, 2001, http://www.sec.gov/news/studies/ordrxmkt.htm.

are trying to serve their investors, and one of the things that they care a lot about is volatility. If you look at volatility on the New York, I want to draw your attention to the following. One, on our Website, we have updated a study of 48 companies that moved to the New York Stock Exchange from NASDAQ. You will find that their volatility gets cut in half. We attribute that to our model, and to how we centralize the order flow and the players in our model. That is important to companies and to issuers, because it lowers their cost of capital. By definition, if you have lower volatility, you will have lower execution costs for investors.

The third point is a lower cost of execution. On this, I will simply rely on the third-party experts – Plexus, Able Noser, and Elkins/McSherry – to deliver our message. Execution costs on the New York Stock Exchange are anywhere between 19 and 49 percent lower that other markets.

In short, we have an infrastructure today that, in our view, is successful. It works. It delivers quality for investors and for the issuers who we are trying to serve. That said, everybody in this room has clearly stated that that is not enough. The New York Stock Exchange must try harder. The challenge for the Exchange is to develop the hybrid model.

When we talk about a hybrid model, you should know that we already have one today on some level. In fact, 99.4 percent of the orders, representing about 63 percent of the volume, are going directly to the specialists. The balance of the volume – 37 percent – is going to brokers. That is a little misleading because it is basically a day's volume divided up. Brokers are handling orders that sometimes are multi-day orders that are not necessarily reflected in those numbers. In any event, the customers have said that they want more. What is the 'more' that they want? How will this hybrid evolve? What are we going to focus on?

Let us come back to the three segments I spoke of earlier. The first is information – namely, the quotations. The first important step is to make the limit order book open and real time. We are working on delivering this very shortly – in a matter of weeks or certainly a couple of months, I hope that we will be up and running with a real time book.[42] With respect to execution services, John Thain has established that we are going to be a fast market. Therefore, Direct+ will largely take over in terms of the dimension of execution.

---

[42] NYSE OpenBook real-time is currently in testing and awaiting SEC approval.

In relation to this, think about the following: If today we are executing 63 percent of the volume that is going to the specialists through DOT, we will be doing that in one or two seconds. What has been your DOT order is now going to become your Direct+ order in terms of execution. We are going to sweep everything through, and see if it is eligible for an execution in real time. We will incorporate marker orders into Direct+, and we will raise the order sizes and eliminate any barriers to a continuous flow of orders through Direct+.

I think that all of this sounds great. We probably can take many of the DOT orders that we have been getting – those 12 million orders that we are getting through DOT today. I suspect that the lion's share of those orders (given that we get a lot of marketable limits today), will be turned into automatic executions. No one will see that, not even the specialists. Those orders will be paired off and reported back to the customers anonymously.

It is important, in creating this hybrid model, that we also create opportunities for the auction to take place. Back at the Exchange, right now, we are trying to figure out the triggers that suggest that it is time for an auction. Is it a price dislocation, a premium, or a discount? Is it the number of shares? What exactly is it that creates this moment when customers and investors would be better served, not by automatic executions, but by taking advantage of discounts or premiums that they think are important in terms of execution.

That is the challenge – to superimpose the auction in places where we need it at any moment. While I think that everybody can agree that the hybrid model has a lot of benefits, its greatest benefit is that it sits there waiting for its opportunity to be effective. You do not know when you are going to need it. You do not know whether there is going to be news. You do not know whether someone is going to restate earnings. You do not know whether there will be an earnings report. You do not have any idea what is going to affect any stock at any moment. It certainly seems to me that you would want an infrastructure that gives protection when you need it.

Institutional Express and Liquidity Quote ought to be reevaluated and examined closely. That brings me back to the question that was asked in the last panel about whether we are going back to block trading. I think that everybody reminisces about the time when they could do a large block trade on the Exchange. There may be a chance to recreate that, but we have to get the fast market Direct+ done first. We have to figure out how to superimpose the auction. And then, to the degree that we can refocus on the specialist and on the marketplace to commit capital again in large size, we may be able to recreate some of those block executions that we have known in the past.

We have to create even more efficient closings. We will start with more electronic adaptation at the close. But we are very efficient today. That is one of our great strengths right now – the opening and closing. Nevertheless, we have to do it even more efficiently. Technology can play a role.

We have also seen and heard from our customers that they would like to have more choices about where they can print their stops and VWAP trades after the market's 4:00 pm markets close. You will see the Exchange introducing something called Crossing III and IV.[43]

Creating that hybrid model also has other important dimensions. We need more transparency around the book. We need better and faster execution capability. We must have the ability to superimpose the auction as we need it, where the brokers and the specialists can add value. We can make the openings and closings more transparent and more efficient. And there is something else as well – with regard to price improvement, how do we reach for better bids and offers, and how do other customers reach our better bids and offers, since we are creating the NBBO 93 percent of the time?

There is unanimity in the view that ITS needs to be either scrapped or changed. We will have to integrate ITS with Direct+, and give automatic executions to those orders that are coming through ITS. But I do not think that it will be free. It is not a sensible business strategy to give our nonmembers better access at lower costs than what we give our members.

As we move forward, you can expect to see the intermarket linkages tightened and becoming more efficient. But they will not be free. They probably will have a fee associated with them that they do not have today. The important point is that the linkages work very efficiently. Ultimately, most of our competitors either are members or have access through a member. Over the next 12 months you will probably see most people coming in the front door as opposed to the side door. Nevertheless, we can make the side door very efficient and effective, both for our competitors and for our customers.

---

[43] Crossing Sessions III and IV debuted on June 15, 2004.

The specialist's responsibilities will be tightened up. We will probably make information about their performance more transparent, not only for specialist units, but for individual specialists. Last but not least, you will see advanced techniques and technology being used to support the specialists' ability to make quotes and to execute trades. Equally important, the other floor brokers will have equivalent technology. They will be making the decisions about when, where, and how to use that technology to compete effectively in a marketplace that includes both floor auctions and execution models like Direct+ and Institutional Express.

There will still be a role for that trusted broker who will provide execution quality to the institution in whatever names the broker thinks are appropriate for his services. You will see specialists doing far less reporting of current market conditions than they are doing today, but much more quoting, committing capital, and taking risks. The whole pace of the market, both at the quote level and at the execution level, will extend to those coming in the front door as well as those coming in the side door.

In a nutshell, we are starting from a very solid platform of success. We can layer on that platform exactly what our customers would like. We can create the hybrid model. That is what the markets expect the New York Stock Exchange to do. We have been very successful in the listed space. We have competed effectively with all types of competitors who have come along, and we will continue to do so. As I said earlier, the Exchange will continue to enhance its trading systems. A more transparent limit order book will be important. The combination of better information about available trading interests and tighter spreads, will all be effective.

I will close by saying that it is not an either/or proposition. It is not electronic or floor. It can be both. Thus far, the fully electronic model has not been the panacea many would say it is. What the New York Stock Exchange has to offer has clearly been shown to have value. It has been a success. I would like to make Bill Donaldson's statement come true – the leadership of our market does indeed depend on realizing the benefits of technology while maintaining the advantages of the floor auction model. We will be working very hard to achieve that.

I would be happy to take questions.

LANNY SCHWARTZ (Philadelphia Stock Exchange) [From the Floor]: I have a question about what you said about ITS. I want to ask about raising the cost for access, in effect, by ITS. Recognizing that nobody knows what will happen with Regulation NMS, one would have thought that the access fee caps in the nondiscrimination provisions would constrain your ability to do that. Even if Regulation NMS does not go into effect as proposed, the spirit of it would give an indication of what the Commission's views are about what you are proposing. Do you have a comment on that?

KINNEY: Frankly, I think that the NMS proposal indicates that they would not care if ITS went away from the proposal. We could move to a place immediately and say, okay, we are going to pull it down. We will get rid of the consortium and everybody will walk away and become members of each other's markets. That would work just fine. Then you will pay whatever cost you have to pay in that market.

That said, there may be, as you think about it, some value to maintaining ITS as a network. As long, that is, as you make it as efficient as you possibly can, which includes eliminating the 30-second wait. But I do not think that it is reasonable to do all of that and then let someone use the system for free. My reading of the access proposal says that you could charge a mil or two mils. That might be a reasonable thought. But there are other ways to accomplish the same end. For instance, the New York Stock Exchange could eliminate it and hook every specialist up to Lava, and scrape everybody's liquidity quickly. What you would lose is the central clearing mechanism that exists today in ITS. This mechanism is probably very cost effective. To the degree that we all want to work on our execution models for people who come in the front door, I am not sure that that would not be a sufficient answer for everybody in the short run. Twelve months from now, there will be better answers.

JAMES ANGEL (Georgetown University) [From the Floor]: One of the contentious issues in Reg NMS is the allocation of the data revenue. What are your thoughts on the formula proposed in Reg NMS, and what kind of formula would you like to have for the allocation of the revenue?

KINNEY: I will give you three answers to that. Number one, our view is that, if the SEC was trying to get at abusive practices by putting out that model, it probably would be much better if they took on those practices like sharing market data revenue and those kinds of things. Two, the formula is complex. I have to confess that we are still working our way through it. Third, a couple years ago, the SEC sponsored a debate with Joel Seligman who was the chair of the SEC Advisory Committee on Market

Information, and they hashed this out.[44] They talked about the best way to handle market data and the revenue streams. We ought to go back to the work that was done there. But we are happy that the SEC wants to take on what we think is the problem – namely, abusive practices like market data rebates. I just wish there was a simpler way to do it.

THOMAS DOYLE (Nutmeg Securities) [From the Floor]: Sometime in the recent past there was a bit of an uproar from the floor constituency about the cost. How is that being managed? What have they to look forward to in a hybrid sort of market future that will make the floor a competitive alternative?

KINNEY: You probably know that we have suspended the technology fee that you are referring to for the brokers and the specialists last year. With John Thain's arrival, we are looking at the full financial model of the Exchange, and I expect that more will come out about it later in the year. But it is clear that we provide a lot of value in the technology.

We were trying to find other revenue streams that would help support both the development and the operation of the technology. It is a valid goal to align value with the customers who are using it. Nevertheless, in the context of a full review of how the Exchange makes its money from the revenue side, and our expenses, with John driving that review, I would reserve judgment about where it is headed.

NINA MEHTA (Traders Magazine) [From the Floor]: You just mentioned, regarding the handling of market data and the revenues streams, that we ought to fall back on the work done there. I am referring to Joe Seligman's report last year. He had those three data consolidation models. Are you referring to one of those, or are you referring to some other aspect of...

KINNEY: Our view is that work has been done on this, that the SEC has made a proposal. And while the model is complex, we applaud them for trying to address the issue. But we would hope that there would be a simpler way. I was not calling out any specific thing or model.

ROBERT SCHWARTZ [From the Floor]: Thank you, Cathy, very much. You have given us all a great deal of information and a lot to think about. This concludes our formal program. Now it is time to invite you, along with all of the rest of us, to our cocktail reception.

---

[44] Report Of The Advisory Committee On Market Information: A Blueprint For Responsible Change, September 14, 2001, Http://Www.Sec.Gov/Divisions/Marketreg/Marketinfo/Finalreport.Htm.

CHAPTER 8: THE ECONOMIC VALUE OF A TRADING FLOOR: EVIDENCE FROM THE AMERICAN STOCK EXCHANGE[45,46]

Puneet Handa, University of Iowa
Associate Professor
Robert Schwartz, Zicklin School of Business, Baruch College
Marvin M. Speiser Professor of Finance
Ashish Tiwari, University of Iowa
Assistant Professor of Finance and Matthew Bucksbaum Research Fellow

I. Introduction

In recent years, the trend in equity market structure has been away from floor based trading to automated floor-less trading systems.[47] But the

---

[46] We would like to thank the American Stock Exchange, especially Brett Redfearn and Russ Monahan, for making the necessary data available to us and for providing technical assistance and information. We are also most grateful to the referee for his or her helpful insights and suggestions. We further thank Bill Christie, Hank Bessembinder, Tom George, Bill Lupien, Deniz Ozenbas, Evan Schulman, George Sofianos, Dan Weaver and seminar participants at Dartmouth College, the OPIM Seminar at the Wharton School, University of Delaware, University of Missouri – Columbia, University of Iowa and the 1999 WFA meetings for their comments and suggestions. All errors remain ours.

[47] The Toronto Stock Exchange closed its trading floor in May 1997. The London Stock Exchange, which has been floor-less since Big Bang in 1996, introduced an electronic limit order book into its quote driven market in 1997. NASDAQ is currently planning to do the same. Floorless, electronic continuous trading now characterizes the equity

two national U.S. stock exchanges, the New York Stock Exchange and the American Stock Exchange, still have trading floors. Is this the result of technological inertia and vested interests, or does the floor have economic value? Our objective in this paper is to assess the economic raision d'être of a trading floor. To this end, we examine trades on the floor of the American Stock Exchange (Amex) and contrast them with trades on Amex's automated Post Execution Reporting (PER) system. We find evidence of intelligent order handling by floor traders which results in reduced execution costs that may offset the higher handling costs of floor trades.[48]

Microstructure economists have in the past paid scant attention to the economic value of a trading floor.[49] Some have simply thought the floor archaic in an electronic environment where participants can work with a bank of computer screens far more easily on the upstairs desks than on the trading floor where space is at a premium.[50] Presumably, the computerization of information dissemination would give electronic trading a strong informational advantage vis-à-vis a floor. Nevertheless, Sofianos and Werner (1997), in their analysis of floor broker participation on the NYSE, find that floor brokers do contribute additional liquidity. Pagano and Röell (1992) point out a further advantage of a floor-based trading system: it gives participants 'the opportunity to observe who trades what with whom, how urgently they seem to want to trade, etc.' (p. 619). There are a number of other ways in which a floor trader may add value: (a) the trader might obtain knowledge of the presence of a contra party, mitigating price impact, (b) the trader could 'round up' multiple counter parties, again cushioning the impact by trading in what may be viewed as a spontaneous call auction, (c) the trader could anticipate periods when liquidity is high and trade more

---

markets of Toronto, Paris, Tokyo, Stockholm, Sidney, Switzerland, Madrid, Frankfurt and elsewhere. In the U.S., new alternative trading systems (commonly referred to as ATSs) and Electronic Communications Networks (ECNs) are also electronic, order driven systems.

[48] It is important to assess liquidity impact costs in light of studies such as Amihud and Mendelson (1986), Brennan and Subrahmanyam (1996), and Amihud, Mendelson and Lauterbach (1997), among others, that have provided evidence of a liquidity premium in asset pricing.

[49] Past research has largely focused on comparing execution costs across various market structures such as auction versus dealer markets. See, for example, Huang and Stoll (1996), Bessembinder and Kaufman (1997) and Venkatraman (2001).

[50] Saul Hansell in the New York Times, March 16, 1998 wrote, 'To compete with electronic markets, the New York Stock Exchange is giving traders on its floors all manner of hand-held computer and communication devices. 'The typical broker on the floor is starting to look like a space cadet,' said Greg Kipness...' (page D5).

often and in larger sizes during such periods, (d) the trader could avoid trading in periods when trading is low, and (e) the trader may possess superior ability to read momentum in the market and to time trades accordingly.

A potential drawback of trading via the floor is that handling costs are higher for orders worked on the floor than for orders delivered electronically through PER, and the fixed cost component may be appreciable.[51] Consequently, the floor may be an attractive venue for large, predominantly institutional participants who are concerned with controlling market impact. PER, on the other hand, may be attractive to small, predominantly retail participants whose orders are not large enough to have market impact or to justify the higher fixed cost component of floor-based order handling.

In this paper, we focus on comparing execution costs across the two venues (PER and the floor) for orders in the same stock matched by stock and trade characteristics such as execution price, order size and trade direction. We restrict ourselves to measuring implicit costs of execution such as realized spreads, quoted spreads and effective spreads.[52] We employ a matched pair technique to control for the self-selection of trades submitted to the floor or to PER by investors, thereby allowing for a more meaningful comparison of execution costs across the two venues.

In our data set (October, 2001 Trade and Quote Data for 973 Amex stocks), 23.40% of the trading volume was initiated by floor brokers. Using the matched pair technique, we find that floor broker timed order handling generally results in lower execution costs. Overall, trades handled by floor brokers have a significantly smaller realized half-spread than do PER trades (-3.06 basis points versus 4.43 basis points). It is interesting to note that the realized half-spread for floor trades is actually negative. The contrast holds for all trade size categories in our sample. In addition, floor trades have a lower effective half-spread compared to PER trades (8.11 basis points versus 10.27 basis points). Finally, the quoted half-spread is also lower when floor orders initiate trades than when PER orders initiate trades (16.23 basis points

---

[51] Explicit commission costs are typically higher for orders that are harder to handle. The fixed cost component is implicit in the fact that a customer must maintain a higher trading volume over time in order for the services of a floor broker to be readily available.

[52] There may be other implicit costs of order handling such as the cost of delayed execution or non-execution that are beyond the scope of this study. In that sense our analysis may be viewed as comparing execution costs across two venues conditional on trade execution.

versus 17.47 basis points). These differences are all statistically significant at the 1% level of significance and are economically meaningful.

Our finding of a lower realized spread for floor trades is robust to controls for the information content of a trade. In specific, we extend the matched pair technique to control for permanent price effects, and continue to find that execution costs are lower on the trading floor. We also examine execution costs for SPDRs (Standard and Poors Depository Receipts), a security that is not subject to information asymmetries. Our findings on SPDRs provide strong confirmation that the execution cost differentials are driven by the relative efficiency of order handling on the floor, rather than by information asymmetries.

We examine the determinants of trade initiation on the floor vs. PER using a probit analysis. Our findings are that the floor trading mechanism is preferred for larger sized trades, on occasions when the order flow is in the direction of the initiating trade (but not following a recent large price change) during morning and late afternoon hours, and for less liquid stocks. We further examine the determinants of execution costs on the trading floor by modeling a floor trader's decision to trade that accounts for the potential selectivity bias in the data.[53] Our major findings are that the execution costs are lower for trades initiated in the direction of the order flow, but are higher for trades following large price changes. Together, these findings suggest that floor traders exhibit strategic behavior, becoming more aggressive in response to a thickening of the book on their own side, and becoming more patient following large pre-trade price changes. It thus appears that floor traders can opportunistically seize liquidity without showing their hands too quickly and that, consequently, using a floor broker is equivalent to placing a 'smart' limit order.' This implies a standard that electronic trading must meet in order to provide an environment that, from the point of view of institutional investors, is competitive with the trading floor. Currently, an increasing number of institutional investors have their own DOT machines and smart order handling systems, and are thereby able, to a limited extent, to handle their orders strategically from their upstairs desks, as they would be worked on the trading floor.[54]

In the next section of this paper, we consider order handling mechanisms and price determination in an electronic continuous trading

---

[53] For further discussion of this approach, see Maddala (1996).

[54] DOT (the NYSE's Designated Order Turnaround system) routes orders directly to specialists' posts on the NYSE trading floor and to the Amex's PER system which brings the orders for Amex stocks to the Amex specialists' posts.

system vs. a floor based continuous market. In Section III, we describe the data and methodology used for the study. In Section IV, we present our empirical results. Section V contains our conclusions.

II. Order handling and price formation

Standard limit and market orders are delivered to the Amex specialists through the Amex's Post Execution Reporting (PER) system. Market orders sent in electronically over PER typically trigger trades immediately. They are directly routed to the specialist who may execute them at the prevailing quote or at an improved price within the quote. Some large institutional investors have DOT machines on their trading desks and send in system orders that are market timed. Predominantly, however, this is not the case.

In contrast, an order may be given to a floor broker to be worked on a 'not held' (NH) basis. The order is called 'NH' because the broker is 'not held' to the price existing at the time of the order's arrival if he or she eventually fills the order at a worse price. Price limits are commonly placed on NH orders. Within these limits, a floor broker has the discretion to market time an NH order. Large floor orders are commonly broken up and presented to the market in smaller tranches in the hope of obtaining more favorable market conditions and in an attempt to minimize price impact.

Having an NH order worked on the floor of an exchange may have important benefits for the investor. By responding to market events as they occur, a floor broker can better control two polar opposite implicit execution costs: (i) the market impact cost of trading a large order too aggressively, and (ii) the opportunity cost of trading it too patiently. One might also use a floor broker to gain access to, and to profit from, the agent's superior information about latent order flow.

Comprehensively viewed, the key service provided by floor traders is the timing, sizing, and pricing of the tranches of an order. We expect floor brokers to time NH orders according to current market conditions. This may, in fact, be an important reason why investors submit orders to the floor. In other words, it may be more difficult to work such orders away from the floor.

The time an order is actually submitted is not observable from our data. Floor traders disclose neither the time an order is received nor the full size of the order. Our tests focus on the liquidity impact cost at the time when part or all of an order triggers a trade. It would be of some interest to examine the spreads prevailing in the market at the time an order is placed but, unfortunately, we are not able to do so. Because floor orders are commonly broken up and presented to the market in smaller tranches, the 'full order' that was initially submitted is generally larger than the 'tranche' that triggers a trade at any point in time. This is of no serious consequence for our analysis; we consider the initial order a package of smaller orders, and focus on the timing of the tranches as they are revealed to the market and turned into trades.

III. The Data and Test Design
A. Data

Our analysis uses October, 2001 non-block trade and quote data for 973 Amex stocks. For each stock (ticker symbol), for each day, we have: (i) the quote file (for each posted quote, the time of the posting, the posting exchange, the bid price posted, the size of the bid, the ask price posted, and the size of the ask); and (ii) the trade file (for each trade, the time the trade was reported executed, identification code for the buy account, the quantity purchased, identification code for the sell account and the quantity sold).

In order to classify trades, we first re-construct the National Best Bid and Offer (NBBO)[55] from the quote file, which is updated each time a new quote is posted by an exchange. In re-constructing the NBBO, we adhere strictly to the Consolidated Tape Association's price, size and time priority rules. We follow tradition by using the Lee-Ready algorithm to infer the initiating party.[56] Hence, our master data file contains trades arranged in chronological order and identified as buyer or seller initiated, the source of the initiating order (floor versus PER), and the NBBO at the time of trade execution.

---

[55] The NBBO consists of the best prevailing bid, the size of the best bid and the exchange posting best bid, and similarly the best prevailing ask, the size of the best ask and the exchange posting the best ask.

[56] The Lee-Ready rule is that if the trade execution price is below the average of the prevailing NBBO bid and ask (the mid-quote), we classify it as buyer-initiated, and if the trade execution price is above the mid-quote we classify it as seller-initiated. If a trade occurs at the mid-quote, we use the tick test: if the execution price occurs on a plus tick or a zero-plus tick (i.e., it is higher than the last non-identical execution price), the trade is classified as buyer initiated, and if the execution price occurs on a minus tick or a zero-minus tick, the trade is classified as seller initiated.

We are concerned about strategic order splitting by traders and its affect on our measure of execution cost. We measure market impact by the price adjustment that occurs after a trade. Because order splitting can impact prices after a floor trade t, it can bias our measure of the market impact of the order that triggered trade t. We have information on broker identification. Thus, we eliminate possibly split trades by using the following heuristic rule: for each trade t, we examine the fifteen trades immediately following it. If a trade during this fifteen-trade interval has the same clearing firm on the same side of the trade as trade t, it is identified as a 'split' trade. If trade t has more than three 'split' trades during the following fifteen-trade interval, we eliminate it from the sample. Our analysis is based on this reduced sample of trade observations.

B. Measuring Execution Costs

Consistent with previous studies [for example, Bessembinder and Kauffman (1997); Huang and Stoll (1996)], we measure the quoted half-spread and the effective half-spread for floor trades and PER trades. Consistent with standard practice, the quoted half-spread is defined as one-half of the ratio of the bid-ask spread to the prevailing midquote. The quoted half-spread is an appropriate measure of execution cost only if trades are assumed to occur at the posted quotes. However, it is not appropriate if trades occur away from the quotes.

The relevant measure in the latter case is the effective half-spread which is usually defined as the ratio of the difference between the execution price and the prevailing midquote, to the midquote. The effective half-spread is an accurate measure of the revenue realized by the liquidity provider (and hence, the cost incurred by the liquidity demander) if the value of the asset is unchanged following the trade. However, there is evidence in the literature that the asset value moves in the direction of the trade following the trade [Hasbrouck (1988), Huang and Stoll (1994)]. In other words, the price increases following a market buy and declines following a market sell. Accordingly, a more accurate measure of the execution cost is the realized half-spread, which is sometimes referred to as the temporary price impact.

Following Huang and Stoll (1996) and Bessembinder and Kaufman (1997), we define the realized half-spread for trade t for stock i as the negative of the logarithmic return from the transaction to the mid-quote at the time of the fifteenth trade after the transaction.[57]

C. Matched Pair Sampling Technique

Our objective is to compare execution costs across the two trading venues, floor and PER. There are, of course, exogenous factors such as stock specific characteristics, order size, trade direction (buy or sell), among others, that impact execution costs. To control for these factors we use a matched pair sampling technique. For each floor trade, we try to locate a matching PER trade. The matching criteria are: (1) trades must be in the same stock, (2) trades must be in the same direction (buy or sell), (3) the execution price of the PER trade must be within 20% of the price of the floor trade, and (4) the size of the PER trade must be within 20% of the size of the floor trade.[58] We present our empirical results by categorizing trades into four groups: trades less than 500 shares, trades between 500 and 999 shares, trades between 1000 and 1499 shares and trades between 1500 and 9999 shares.

D. Determinants of Trade Initiation on Floor vs. PER

Our hypothesis is that trades executed on the floor are strategically timed to account for order characteristics and to coincide with market conditions that reduce execution costs. We first focus on understanding the determinants of trade initiation on the two venues. Theoretical research on order submission strategies suggests two variables that may be of particular relevance to our study.   The first explanatory variable, order size, is suggested by theoretical models such as Easley and O'Hara (1987). The second explanatory variable, order imbalance, is suggested by market microstructure models such as Kyle (1985) and Admati and Pfleiderer (1988). Glosten and Harris (1988), Madhavan, Richardson and Roomans (1997) and Huang and Stoll (1997) provide evidence that trade indicator

---

[57] Our definition of temporary price impact incorporates one-half of the spread prevailing at the time of trade execution, a component that we refer to as the spread-related component of price impact. As a test of robustness, we also measured temporary price impact using the mid-quote for trade t to assess the component that is not spread related. The results were generally consistent with the findings reported here.

[58] A similar matched pair technique is also used by Venkatraman (2001) and Conrad et al. (2001).

variables (buyer-initiated and seller-initiated trades) also explain intra-day price movements.

To obtain a measure of order imbalance for a trade t, we begin by dividing each day into 15-minute intervals. Order imbalance for trade t is the aggregate trading volume triggered by orders on the same side of the market (as the order that triggered trade t) relative to total trading volume in the stock over the contemporaneous 15-minute interval.[59] To ensure that the measure is not contaminated by a trader's own trading volume in that 15-minute interval, in computing the imbalance we eliminate all trades that the same trader participates in during that period. Hence, we define the order imbalance for trade t as

$$Imb_t = \frac{Own\text{-}side\ 15\text{-}minute\ trading\ volume}{Total\ 15\text{-}minute\ trading\ volume}$$

For trading intervals during which no trades are recorded for a stock we set Imbt equal to 0.50.

It is possible to identify other variables that may affect the order submission strategy. For example, implementing a momentum strategy requires that one react more aggressively to price changes compared to a value strategy.[60] Hence, recent price changes may be a relevant factor in our analysis. We capture this by incorporating the pre-trade price change as an explanatory variable in our model. Additionally, the time of day may influence order placement. In particular, as the afternoon progresses, we expect to see participants stepping forward to trade because they do not want to risk carrying unfilled orders into the overnight period. We control for the time of the day effect by dividing the trading day into three periods; an opening period (9:30 AM to 10:00 AM), a mid-day period (10:00 AM to 3:30 PM), and a closing period (3:30 PM to 4:00 PM).

---

[59] Our results are robust to several alternative measures of order imbalance. For example, we also examine the ratio of the depth on own side of the book to the total depth at the both prevailing inside quotes. Our concern with the latter measure is that it could be corrupted by the possibility of the floor trader's own order being reflected in the quotes. Nevertheless, the two measures gave very similar results. We also found that changing the length of the window over which imbalance is measured to 5 minutes does not materially alter our results.

[60] We thank the referee for this suggestion.

We formally model the probability of a trade occurring on PER as follows:

$$\Pr(y_t = 0) = \Phi(\theta' z_t)$$

where $\theta' z_t = \theta_0 + \theta_1 q_{1t} + \theta_2 q_{2t} + \theta_3 q_{3t} + \theta_4 Imb_t$
$+ \theta_5 Preret_t + \theta_6 D_{1t} + \theta_7 D_{2t} + \theta_8 Vol_t$

(1)

The variable q_{1t} is a binary indicator variable that takes a value of 1 if the order size is between 500 and 999 shares and zero otherwise, q_{2t} takes a value of 1 if the order size is between 1000 and 1499 shares, and q_{3t} takes a value of 1 if the order size is between 1500 and 9999 shares. The variable Imbt captures the trading imbalance in the market, taking a value closer to zero (one) when there is less (more) trading interest on the side of the initiating trade. The variable Prerett is defined as the absolute value of the return from the mid-quote prevailing fifteen trades prior to trade t, to trade t. The variable D_{1t} is a binary indicator variable that takes a value of 1 if the trade occurs between 9:30 AM and 10 AM and zero otherwise, and D_{2t} takes a value of 1 if the trade occurs between 3:30 PM and 4 PM and zero otherwise. The variable Volt is the logarithm of the average daily trading volume during October 2001 for the stock being traded.

E. Determinants of Execution Costs with Endogenous Trade Initiation by Floor Traders

We now turn to an analysis of the determinants of execution costs for floor trades when floor traders may time orders to minimize realized costs. To handle the potential selection bias in the data, we model the traders' decision to initiate trades, i.e., the decision to submit or withhold an order given the order characteristics and market conditions. Our model follows the standard treatment of cases involving selection bias with an endogenous event.[61] It is similar in spirit to Madhavan and Cheng (1997) who use an endogenous switching regression model to study the price impact of block trades across two venues, namely, the upstairs market and the downstairs market. Both models represent the treatment of cases where data are generated by the self-selection of traders, i.e., by the endogenous choices made by the traders. However, there are important differences. Madhavan and Cheng model the choice of the appropriate venue by an agent and use a two-stage procedure to estimate the model by using data on block trades executed on both venues. In contrast, we analyze the determinants of the realized half-spread for floor trades by modeling a floor trader's decision to execute trades selectively. Since we use data on executed floor trades, two-stage estimation methods are not appropriate in our context. Accordingly, we use the maximum likelihood method to estimate our model.

In our model, the floor trader's decision to initiate trades is dependent on the expected realized half-spread of a trade. Consider a trader who initiates trade t (for simplicity, let t also denote that trader) and who faces a realized half-spread r_t^f. We express the realized half-spread as:

$$r_t^f = \beta_0^f + \beta_{11}^f q_{1t} + \beta_{12}^f q_{2t} + \beta_{13}^f q_{3t} + \beta_2^f Imb_t +$$
$$\beta_3^f Preret_t + \beta_{41}^f D_{1t} + \beta_{42}^f D_{2t} + \beta_5^f Vol_t + \varepsilon_t^f$$

(2)

where ε_t^f is a stochastic error term with variance σ^2. The explanatory variables are as defined under equation 1. The order size indicator variables q_{it} control for the variations in realized half-spread related to the size of the order that the market has to absorb. The order imbalance variable Imb_t controls for variations in execution costs relative to the costs of waiting. The variable $Preret_t$ controls for the impact of recent price changes on order placement. The time-of-day indicator variables D_{1t} and D_{2t} account for intra-day effects. The variable Vol_t is a proxy measure of the general level

---

[61] See Maddala (1996) for examples of such applications in Finance.

of liquidity of the stock and is expected to be an important determinant of the execution cost.[62]

Note that equation (2) could not be estimated using standard OLS procedures if floor traders endogenously time their trades. In this case, the data would be subject to a selectivity bias. Hence, the OLS procedure would yield inconsistent parameter estimates since the conditional means of the observed error terms in equation (2) would be non-zero.

We expect a floor trader to initiate a trade if and only if the expected realized half-spread is below a threshold level.[63] We define the latent variable y_t^* as the expected difference between the realized half-spread for trader t and the threshold value ct:

$$y_t^* = E\left[\left(r_t^f - c_t\right)\middle|\Omega_t\right] + \xi_t$$

(3)

where Ωt is the information set for trader t and ξ_t denotes an error term with variance normalized to 1. We can write the above equation in compact form as:

$$y_t^* = \gamma' z_t + \xi_t$$

(4)

where zt is the vector of explanatory variables outlined in equation (1), and γ is the vector of coefficients.[64] Floor trader t chooses to step forward with an order if $y_t^* \leq 0$, otherwise the trader withholds the order. Let y_t

---

[62] There are other possible proxies of a stock's liquidity such as price level, value of shares outstanding, etc. In our tests we found these variables to be highly correlated with a stock's trading volume.

[63] The threshold value can be viewed as a constant. A more general interpretation is possible, however. It can be viewed as the cost of waiting to trade later and hence, as a function of the order characteristics and market conditions at the time of the decision. The model estimates are unaffected by the interpretation.

[64] In other words,

$$\gamma' z_t = \gamma_0 + \gamma_1 q_{1t} + \gamma_2 q_{2t} + \gamma_3 q_{3t} + \gamma_4 Imb + \gamma_5 Preret + \gamma_6 D_{1t} + \gamma_7 D_{2t} + \gamma_8 Vol$$

represent a variable that takes the value 1 if the trader chooses to trade and takes the value 0 otherwise. Hence, the observable variable is:

$$y_t = \begin{cases} 1 & if\ y_t^* \leq 0 \\ 0 & if\ y_t^* > 0 \end{cases}$$

(5)

We assume that $\left(\varepsilon_t^f, \xi_t\right)$ are jointly normally distributed with means zero and covariance matrix Σ, where:

$$\Sigma = \begin{bmatrix} \sigma^2 & \rho\sigma \\ \rho\sigma & 1 \end{bmatrix}$$

(6)

Using the properties of the normal distribution, we can write the expected realized half-spread conditional on observing a floor trade as:[65]

$$E\left(r_t^f \middle| y^* \leq 0\right) = \beta_0^f + \beta_{11}^f q_{1t} + \beta_{12}^f q_{2t} + \beta_{13}^f q_{3t} + \beta_2^f Imb + + \beta_3^f Preret +$$

$$\beta_{41}^f D_{1t} + \beta_{42}^f D_{2t} + \beta_5^f Vol + \rho\sigma\left[\frac{-\phi(\gamma'z_t)}{1-\Phi(\gamma'z_t)}\right]$$

(7)

Re-writing equation (7) in compact notation, we get:

$$E\left(r_t^f \middle| y^* \leq 0\right) = X_i\beta + \rho\sigma\left[\frac{-\phi(\gamma'z_t)}{1-\Phi(\gamma'z_t)}\right]$$

(8)

---

[65] See Maddala (1983).

where ϕ and Φ are, respectively, the density function and the cumulative distribution function of the standard normal (evaluated at $\gamma' z_i$) and ρ is the correlation between ε_i^f and ξ_i. Note that in the absence of self-selection of orders by the traders, ρ would be equal to zero. This allows us to test the null hypothesis that traders do not time their orders.

We use data on executed floor trades for our analysis. Equation (8) is estimated by maximizing the following likelihood function that takes into account the truncated nature of the data:[66]

$$L = \prod_i [\Phi(-Z_i\gamma)]^{-1} \frac{1}{\sigma} \exp\left[-\frac{1}{2\sigma^2}(y_i - X_i\beta)^2\right] \times \Phi\left(\frac{-[Z_i\gamma - \rho(y_i - X_i\beta)/\sigma]}{(1-\rho^2)^{1/2}}\right)$$

(9)

IV. Results
  A. Characteristics of Trades Executed on the Amex

Table 1 (page 148) presents descriptive statistics for the trades in the sample we have analyzed.

Overall, the volume of trades initiated on the floor is 110,489,600, accounting for 23.40% of the total volume. Trading volume initiated on PER accounts for 361,739,540 shares traded, or 76.60% of total volume. In addition to the 23.40% trading volume reported in Table 1 that is initiated on the floor, there is an additional 10.39% trading volume in which the trading floor is a passive participant. It is clear that the trading floor is an attractive venue for many non-block trades. Henceforth, we refer to trades initiated on the floor as floor trades and those initiated on PER as PER trades. We classify trades into four categories according to the number of shares transacted at the trade: (i) less than 500 shares, (ii) between 500 and 999 shares, (iii) between 1000 and 1499 shares, and (iv) between 1500 and 9,999 shares.

For trades less than 500 shares, floor trades account for only 3.96 million shares (0.84% of total trading volume) and PER trades account for 58.54 million shares (12.40% of total trading volume). The average size of floor trades in this category is 283.76 shares. For PER trades, the average

---

[66] For details, please see pages 266-267, Maddala (1983).

size is slightly smaller at 250.54 shares. As may be seen from the last panel of Table 1, the average time spanned by the thirty trades surrounding a typical trade of less than 500 shares is 30.54 minutes. For floor trades, this time span is marginally more than the time span for PER trades.

There are 73.47 million shares traded in the 500-999 trade size category. Floor trades account for 8.50 million shares (1.80% of the total trading volume) while PER trades account for the remainder 64.97 million shares (13.76% of total trading volume). The average size of floor trades is 905.19 shares. For PER trades, the average size is again slightly smaller at 882.46 shares. The average time spanned by the thirty trades surrounding a typical trade of between 500 shares and 999 shares is 26.07 minutes.

There are only 27.48 million shares traded in the 1000-1500 trade size category. Of these, floor trades account for 4.72 million shares (1.00% of total trading volume) while PER trades account for 22.77 million shares (4.82% of total trading volume). As in the other categories, PER trades are smaller-sized with an average of 1346.59 shares compared to floor trades (1358.08 shares). The average time spanned by the thirty trades surrounding a typical trade in this category is 27.74 minutes.

Finally, for the trades between 1500 and 9999 shares, floor trades account for 93.31 million shares (19.76% of total trading volume) and PER trades account for 215.46 million shares (45.63% of trading volume). The average size of floor trades of between 1500 shares and 9999 shares is 4038.46 shares. For PER trades, the average size is considerably smaller at 3366.31 shares. The average time spanned by the thirty trades surrounding a typical trade in this category is only 21.34 minutes.

B. Evidence on execution costs

Table 2 (page 149) presents our measures of execution costs for a matched sample of floor and PER trades. Using the matching criteria discussed in Section III C, we were able to find a matching PER trade for 48,471 floor trades out of a total of 49,940 floor trades (i.e., 97.06%). The matching procedure led to a close match between the trade pairs. Namely, the mean difference in trade execution price between the pairs was 7.04% with a median difference of 5.26%, and the mean difference in trade size between the pairs was 7.09% with a median difference of 2.44%. We present evidence on the following measures of execution cost: the quoted half-spread, the effective half-spread and the realized half-spread. The trades are classified into four trade size categories: less than 500 shares, 500 - 999 shares, 1000 – 1499 shares and 1500 - 9999 shares.

Panel 1 of the table presents evidence on the quoted half-spread. Overall, the floor trade sample has an average quoted half-spread of 16.23 basis points as compared to 17.49 basis points for the matched PER trade sample. The difference of -1.24 basis points is significant at the 1% level of significance. In terms of trade size categories, the quoted half-spread is significantly lower for floor trades in all of the categories. The difference varies from -0.84 basis points for large trades to -2.56 basis points for the 1000-1499 shares category.

As stated earlier, the quoted half-spread reflects the true execution cost only if trades occur at the quotes. In panel 2, we present evidence on the effective half-spread. The effective half-spread is consistently lower for floor trades across all categories, and averages 8.11 basis points as compared to 10.27 basis points for a matched sample of PER trades. The difference of negative 2.16 basis points is significant at the 1% level of significance. It varies from -1.57 basis points for large trades to -2.89 basis points for the 500-999 shares category. It is significant at the 1% level for all cases.

In panel 3, we present evidence on the realized half-spread. As discussed previously, the realized half-spread is the most appropriate measure of the compensation realized by a liquidity provider, and hence, the cost to a liquidity seeker. The realized half-spread is consistently lower for floor trades, averaging -3.06 basis points compared to 4.43 basis points for the matched sample of PER trades. The difference of -7.49 basis points is significant at the 1% level. This difference is negative and significant for each of the trade-size categories. It is interesting to note that the realized spread on floor orders is consistently negative for all trade categories. This suggests that, with effective order handling, trading gains may be realized instead of market impact costs being incurred.

At this stage it is worthwhile to ask whether the differences in execution costs across the two venues are economically meaningful. To assess this issue we can compare the difference in execution costs to the mean quoted half-spread of 16.85 bps in our matched sample. The differences in realized half-spreads reported in Panel 3 translate to between 36.38 percent and 57.63 percent of the mean quoted half-spread. This suggests that differential execution costs are appreciable, and that trading on the more expensive venue can aggregate into major dollar costs for investors. Alternatively stated, bringing orders to the floor can generate savings that justify the higher fees that floor access involves.

The evidence on realized half-spreads is consistent with the hypothesis that floor traders time their orders to minimize execution costs, by buying (selling) at times of rising (falling) stock prices. This would explain why, in equilibrium, some trades would be submitted to the trading floor in spite of higher access costs (that are not measured in this study). An alternative interpretation of these findings is that floor trades have higher information content. In the next section, we seek to distinguish between these two hypotheses.

C. Evidence on Execution Costs of Trades with Similar Information
    Content

We refine our matching technique to control for the information content of trades. Specifically, we expand the matching criteria to include a control for the Permanent Price Impact of a trade defined as:

$$Permanent\ Price\ Impact = D_{it} \cdot \left[\ln\left(\frac{M_{+15}}{M_{-15}} \right) \right]$$

where D_{it} is an indicator variable that is equal to +1 for buyer-initiated trades and is equal to –1 for seller-initiated trades, and M_{+15} (M_{-15}) refers to the mid-quote prevailing at the time of the fifteenth trade after (before) trade t. The permanent price impact is a measure of the information content of a trade (see, for example, Kraus and Stoll (1972), and Madhavan and Cheng (1997)).

In addition to the previous matching criteria, we now require the permanent price impact of PER trades to be within 20% of the permanent price impact of floor trades. With this constraint we obtain matching PER trades for 45,536 floor trades (i.e., 91.18% of all floor trades). The mean difference in the trade execution price between the pairs is 6.79% with a median difference of 5.69%. The mean difference in trade size between the pairs is 6.70% with a median difference of 0. Finally, the mean difference in permanent price impact between the pairs is 9.66% with a median difference of 9.64%.

We present measures of the execution cost for this reduced sample of matched trades in Table 3 (page 150). The first panel in the table presents the quoted half-spreads for the matched sample of floor trades and PER trades classified by four trade size categories. The average quoted half-spread for floor trades is 14.53 basis points as compared to 15.38 basis points for PER trades. The difference of –0.85 basis points is significant at the 1% level. Additionally, floor trades have significantly lower quoted half-spreads for each of the four trade-size categories.

Results on effective half-spreads are presented in the second panel of the table. Similar to the results for the full sample in Section 3.2, effective half-spreads for floor trades average 7.13 basis points as compared to 8.94 basis points for the matched sample of PER trades. The difference of -1.81 basis points is significant at the 1% level of significance. Also, it is significantly negative for all the trade size categories, varying from -1.15 basis points for the large trade category to -2.64 basis points for the 500-999 share category.

In the third panel of the table, we present results on the realized half-spreads. Overall, realized half-spreads for floor trades average -4.21 basis points as compared to -0.09 basis points for PER trades. The difference of –4.12 basis points is significant at the 1% level of significance. The difference is significantly negative for individual trade size categories. Once again, realized spreads are negative for floor trades in all trade size categories, varying from -2.88 basis points for large trades to -6.68 basis points for the 1000-1499 share category. Also, the realized spread is negative for the PER small trades at -2.55 basis points.

Overall, the results for the sample where we control for the permanent price impact are similar to the results for the full sample. We note, however, that, with just one exception, for all three half-spread measures and four size categories for both floor and PER orders, the half-spread values are somewhat smaller when we control for the permanent price impact. A higher information content of floor trades could account for this. Nevertheless, all measures of execution costs shown in Table 3, including the quoted half-spread, the effective half-spread and the realized half-spread, are significantly lower for the floor trades. This suggests that we can rule out information differences as the main reason for the lower realized half-spreads for floor trades. We further test the information content hypothesis by focusing on SPDRs, a security for which we expect no meaningful informational asymmetries.

D. Evidence on Execution Costs of Trades for SPDRS

The Amex's SPDRs (Standard and Poors Depository Receipts) are an exchange traded fund (ETF), that is potentially subject to little or no information asymmetry.[67] A SPDR represents an ownership interest in the SPDR trust that holds all of the S&P 500 composite stocks, and is a highly liquid alternative to the S&P index mutual funds. SPDRs offer us an opportunity to compare execution costs across the floor and PER in a setting that is largely devoid of private information. A finding that execution costs are different across the two venues for SPDR trades would further confirm the hypothesis that these cost differentials are driven by the relative efficiency of order handling in the two venues, rather than by informational asymmetries.

Table 4 (page 151) presents the evidence on execution costs for SPDRS. The first panel in the table presents the quoted half-spreads for the matched sample of floor trades and PER trades classified by four trade size categories. The average quoted half-spread for floor trades is 3.93 basis points as compared to 4.01 basis points for PER trades. The difference of – 0.08 basis points is not significant. Floor trades have lower quoted half-spreads for the larger trade size categories but a higher quoted spread for the less than 500 share trade size category. Even though the differences in these two categories are statistically significant, they do not appear to be economically meaningful.

Results on effective half-spreads are presented in the second panel of the table. Effective half-spreads for floor trades average 0.95 basis points as compared to 2.23 basis points for the matched sample of PER trades. The difference of –1.27 basis points is significant at the 1% level. Also, it is significantly negative for each of the individual trade size categories.

In the third panel of the table, we present results on the realized half-spreads. Overall, realized half-spreads for floor trades average -0.09 basis points as compared to 2.06 basis points for PER trades. The difference of – 2.16 basis points is negative and significant at the 1% level. Also, the difference is consistently negative and significant at the 1% level across all trade size categories. To benchmark these results, note that the mean quoted half-spread in our matched sample is 3.97 bps. Hence, the differences in realized half-spread that we report in Panel 3, range from 47.36 % to 70.03% of the mean quoted half-spread.

---

[67] SPDRs are now also traded on the NYSE.

In contrast to our full sample of stocks, the quoted half-spreads and effective half-spreads for SPDRS are substantially smaller across the board. This is also true for the realized half-spread for SPDR PER trades (though not for floor trades). This finding is consistent with the absence of any meaningful informational asymmetries for SPDRs. Despite absence of information asymmetries, we observe differences between the execution costs of floor and PER trades reported in Table 4 that are consistent with our earlier findings. This strongly suggests that the trading floor offers the advantage of lower execution costs through improved order handling.

E. Evidence on Determinants of Order Arrival on Floor vs. PER

We present below the probit estimates based on equation (1) (chi-square statistics are in parenthesis):

$$\theta z_t = \begin{array}{l} 0.9031 - 0.4037\ q_{1t} - 0.6578\ q_{2t} - 1.0240\ q_{3t} - 0.2094\ Imb_t \\ (31060)\quad (32208)\quad (34217)\quad (26378)\quad (66225) \end{array}$$

$$+ 6.0362\ Preret - 0.0093D_{1t} - 0.0207D_{2t} + 0.0864\ Vol$$
$$\quad (28020)\qquad (1.14)\qquad (5.39)\qquad (279518)$$

LogLikelihood= -1409889619

$$(10)$$

The coefficients on the three order size indicator variables are all significantly negative, indicating that larger sized orders have a lower probability of being executed on PER and, therefore, a greater probability of execution on the floor. The coefficient on the variable Imbt is significantly negative, suggesting that, as own-side order imbalance increases, there is a lower probability of a PER trade and, correspondingly, a higher probability of a floor-based trade. The co-efficient on the variable Prerett is significantly positive, indicating that a PER trade is more likely following a large pre-trade price change. The findings on Imbt and Prerett imply that floor traders observe and react to order imbalance and that floor trades are more likely when there is more interest on the side of the initiating trade. At the same time, floor traders appear to be relatively patient and to avoid trading after large pre-trade price changes. Later on we show that this behavior is consistent with minimizing execution costs. Conversely, PER traders appear more apt to chase price changes (i.e., to engage in momentum trading), which may explain our earlier findings of higher realized half-spreads for PER trades.[68]

The morning time-of-day indicator variable (D1t) has a negative but insignificant co-efficient, and the late afternoon time-of-day indicator variable (D2t) has a significantly negative co-efficient. This indicates that, relative to mid-day, floor trades are more likely in the morning and afternoon. There are two factors at play here: (1) there is evidence that the markets are more liquid during the morning and afternoon hours than during mid-day [see, for example, Jain and Joh (1988)], and (2) floor traders who may be willing to be patient earlier in the trading day, are more apt to step forth and trade as the closing bell approaches so as to avoid carrying an open position into the overnight period.

Finally, the coefficient on average trading volume is significantly positive, implying that the probability of a PER trade increases with the average trading volume of the stock (that is a measure of the stock's liquidity). Conversely, for a given order size, a less liquid stock that requires more special order handling is more likely to be traded via the floor.

In sum, the probit estimates suggest that the floor trading mechanism is preferred for larger sized trades, on occasions when the book is thicker on the side of the trade initiating order (but not following a recent large price change), during the late afternoon hours and for less liquid stocks.

F.   Evidence on Determinants of Execution Costs

The estimates of the trade initiation model given by equation (8) are presented below:

---

[68] Keim and Madhavan (1995) show that traders following momentum-based strategies trade more aggressively and incur higher trading costs relative to value traders.

$$E\left(r_t^f \mid y^* \leq 0\right) = 0.00003^* + 0.00042^{***} q_{1t} + 0.00037^* q_{2t} + 0.00063^{***} q_{3t}$$

$$-0.00399^{***} Imb_t + .06184^{**} Preret_t - 0.00046^{***} D_{1t} + 0.0001 D_{2t}$$

$$+ 0.00014^{***} Vol_t + 0.08683 \left[\frac{-\hat{\phi}(\gamma' Z_t)}{1 - \hat{\Phi}(\gamma' Z_t)} \right]$$

$$(11)$$

where

$$\gamma' Z_t = 0.60402 - 0.18755 q_{1t} + 0.50145^{***} q_{2t} + 0.79156^{***} q_{3t}$$

$$+ 0.72311^* Imb_t + 0.13271 Preret_t + 0.26139^{***} D_{1t} + 0.15004 D_{2t}$$

$$+ 1.48472^{**} Vol_t$$

$$(12)$$

***   indicates significance at the 1% level ;
**   indicates significance at the 5% level;
*   indicates significance at the 10% level.

In equation (11), the co-efficients corresponding to the second through the fourth terms (corresponding to the order-size indicator variables q1t, q2t and q3t) are significantly positive, which indicates that the expected realized half-spread increases with order size. In contrast, the co-efficient of Imbt in equation (11) is significantly negative, implying that the expected realized half-spread decreases with order imbalance. The co-efficient for Prerett in equation (11) is significantly positive, implying that the expected realized half-spread increases following recent price changes. The results on Imbt and Prerett in conjunction with our earlier Probit results, suggest strategic behavior on the part of floor traders who become more aggressive in response to a thickening of the book on their own side, and who become patient following large pre-trade price changes.

The co-efficient of the morning dummy variable D1t in equation (11) is significantly negative, implying that the expected realized half-spread is low in the morning hours, at a time when we expect market liquidity to be higher. The co-efficient of the afternoon dummy variable D2t is positive but insignificant. Given our earlier probit results that the probability of floor initiated trades is higher in the afternoons, it appears that, as the day wears on, the traders' patience wears thin and the desire to complete their orders increases. Finally, the co-efficient of average trading volume is positive and significant, which would suggest that the expected cost of trading via the floor is higher for larger volume stocks, and that the floor is a relatively more attractive venue for less liquid stocks. The last term of equation (11) is commonly referred to as the Inverse Mills ratio. The co-efficient of this term is insignificant, which indicates that selectivity bias may be absent in the data.[69]

Similarly, the results in equation (12) are economically insightful. The equation presents the relationship between the probability of a floor trade occurring (as opposed to a trade being withheld) and order size, order imbalance, recent price change, time of day and average trading volume for the stock. This probability increases with order size except for the small share category, for which the co-efficient is insignificant. The probability of a floor trade increases with order imbalance as well. With respect to price changes, the results are insignificant. With respect to the time-of-day, floor trades are more likely in the morning hours. The results are insignificant with respect to the late afternoon. The results are consistent with more liquidity being available in the morning. Finally, the probability of a floor trade increases with average trading volume, indicating that floor traders are more inclined to trade a stock with higher average trading volume quickly than they are to trade a stock with lower average trading volume. As one would expect, more strategic behavior is required for stocks with lower average trading volume.

---

[69] Following this finding, we estimated equation (2) using OLS, and the sign and significance of the explanatory variables was virtually identical to those in equation (11).

V. Conclusion

For an expanding array of equity markets, including Toronto, Paris, Tokyo, Australia, Madrid, Stockholm, Switzerland, Frankfurt and London, floorless electronic trading systems have been the wave of the future. In this paper, we have focused on the value of a trading floor. Our analysis of non-block trades on the Amex, a floor-based market, suggests that the floor environment adds value through improved order handling. Consistent with this, we find that 23.40% of the trading volume in our sample is initiated on the trading floor and that, on the passive side, the floor participates in an additional 10.39% of the trading volume.

Using a matched pair technique, we find that floor broker timed order handling generally results in lower execution costs. Overall, trades handled by floor brokers have a significantly smaller realized half-spread than do PER trades (-3.06 basis points versus 4.43 basis points). This difference of 7.49 basis points is equivalent to a savings of 3.94 cents per share for an average priced stock on the Amex.[70] Given the aggregate floor trading volume of 110,489,600 shares in October 2001, this translates to a total savings of $4.36 million for the month. In addition, floor trades have a lower effective half-spread compared to PER trades (8.11 basis points versus 10.27 basis points). The quoted half-spread is also lower when floor orders initiate trades than when PER orders initiate trades (16.23 basis points versus 17.47 basis points).

Our finding of a lower realized spread for floor trades is robust to controls for the information content of a trade. In specific, we examine execution costs for a restricted sample that further controls for the permanent price effect. We continue to find that execution costs are lower on the trading floor.

Our evidence on SPDRs, a security that is not subject to information asymmetries, further reinforces the above findings. We find that execution costs continue to be lower on the floor despite absence of information differentials for matched trades compared across the two venues.

Our findings on SPDRs strongly suggest that the trading floor offers the advantage of reduced execution costs through improved order handling.

We have examined the determinants of trade initiation on the floor vs. PER. Our findings are that the floor trading mechanism is preferred for

---

[70] In this context, we define the average price as the trade-weighted transaction price in our sample.

larger sized trades, on occasions when the order flow is in the direction of the initiating trade (but not following a recent large price change), during morning and late afternoon hours, and for less liquid stocks. Our findings on the determinants of execution costs on the trading floor are that the execution costs are lower for trades initiated in the direction of the order flow, but higher for trades that are preceded by large price changes.

Together, these findings suggest that floor traders exhibit strategic behavior, becoming more aggressive in response to a thickening of the book on their own side, and becoming more patient following large pre-trade price changes. In contrast, PER traders are more apt to chase recent price changes. This helps explain why floor orders incur lower (and even negative) execution costs and sheds light on the role of floor brokers and the value of intermediation in an equity market.

It is important to point out, however, that, to some extent at least, the functions of a floor trader can be carried out in an electronic environment, and that the strategic timing of trades does not necessarily require verbal order entry by human intermediaries. A growing number of institutional investors now have DOT machines and smart order handling systems that give them some ability to work their orders strategically from their upstairs desks. The ECNs show orders away from the best bid and offer (as the New York Stock Exchange now does through its Open Book), and some of the ECNs have reserve book functionality. While this may not yet be enough for buy-side traders working their own smart limit orders to compete with floor traders handling not held orders,[71] with improvements in the technology for order routing and handling and the development of superior market design, one might expect the future to lie with electronic trading.

Observing that trading costs can be controlled by proper trade initiation underscores the need to design an environment that best presents the relevant information on market conditions to participants. Our analysis suggests a standard that the electronic platforms must meet, especially with regard to institutional order flow.

---

[71] For further discussion of this point, see Keim and Madhavan (1996).

REFERENCES

Admati, A., and Pfleiderer, P. 1988. A theory of intraday patterns: volume and price variability. Review of Financial Studies 1: 3-40.

Amihud, Yakov, and Mendelson, Haim 1986. Asset pricing and the bid-ask spread. Journal of Financial Economics 17: 223-249.

Amihud, Yakov, Mendelson, Haim, and Lauterbach, Beni 1997. Market microstructure and securities values: Evidence from the Tel Aviv Stock Exchange. Journal of Financial Economics 45: 365-390.

Bessembinder, H., and Kaufman, H.M. 1997. A cross-exchange comparison of execution costs and information flow for NYSE-listed stocks. Journal of Financial Economics 46: 293-319.

Brennan, M., and Subrahmanyam, A. 1996. Market microstructure and asset pricing: on the compensation for illiquidity in stock returns. Journal of Financial Economics 41: 441-464.

Conrad, Jennifer, Johnson, Kevin M., and Wahal, Sunil 2001. Alternative Trading Systems. Working Paper, Emory University.

Easley, David, and O'Hara, Maureen 1987. Price, trade size and information in securities markets. Journal of Financial Economics 19: 69-90.

Glosten, L., and Harris, L. 1988. Estimating the components of the bid/ask spread. Journal of Financial Economics 21: 123-142.

Huang, Roger D., and Stoll, Hans R. 1994. Market microstructure and stock return predictions: A paired comparison of execution costs on NASDAQ and the NYSE. Review of Financial Studies 7: 179-213.

Huang, Roger D., and Stoll, Hans R. 1996. Dealer versus auction markets: A paired comparison of execution costs on NASDAQ and the NYSE. Journal of Financial Economics 41: 313-357.

Huang, Roger D., and Stoll, Hans R. 1997. The components of the bid-ask spread: a general approach. Review of Financial Studies 10: 995-1034.

Jain, Prem, and Joh, Gun-Ho 1988. The dependence between hourly prices and trading volume. Journal of Financial and Quantitative Analysis 23: 269-284.

Keim, D. B., and Madhavan, A. 1995. The Anatomy of the Trading Process. Journal of Financial Economics 37: 391-398.

Keim, Donald B., and Madhavan, Ananth 1996. The upstairs market for large-block transactions: analysis and measurement of price effects. Review of Financial Studies 9: 1-36.

Kraus, A., and Stoll, H. 1972. Price impacts of block trading on the New York Stock Exchange. Journal of Finance 27: 569-588.

Kyle, A. 1985. Continuous auctions and insider trading. Econometrica 53: 1315-1335.

Lee, Charles, and Ready, Mark 1991. Inferring trade direction from intraday data. Journal of

Finance 46: 733-746.

Maddala, G.S. 1983. Li mited dependent and qualitative variables in econometrics. New York: Cambridge University Press.

Maddala, G.S. 1996. Applications of the limited dependent variable models in finance. In G.S. Maddala and C.R. Rao (eds.), Handbook of Statistics 14: 553-566. Elsevier Science B.V.

Madhavan, Ananth, and Cheng, M. 1997. In search of liquidity: block trades in the upstairs and downstairs markets. Review of Financial Studies 10: 175-204.

Madhavan, Ananth, Richardson, M., and Roomans, M. 1997. Why do security prices change? A transaction-level analysis of NYSE stocks. Review of Financial Studies 10: 1035-1064.

Pagano, Marco, and Röell, Ailsa 1992. Auction and dealership markets: what is the difference? European Economic Review 36: 613-623.

Sofianos, George and Werner, Ingrid M. 1997. The trades of NYSE floor brokers, Working Paper. New York Stock Exchange.

Venkataraman, Kumar 2001. Automated versus floor trading: An analysis of execution costs on the Paris and New York exchanges. Journal of Finance 56: 1445-1485.

Table 1

Sample Statistics

Share volume, percent of volume, trade size and time between trades for the four trade size categories at the American Stock Exchange during October 2001

We classify both floor initiated and PER initiated trades into four categories: less than 500 shares, between 500 and 999 shares, between 1000 and 1499 shares, and between 1500 and 9999 shares. Number of trades, Percent of Trades (%), Trade size (shares), and Time between Trades −15 to +15 (in minutes) is reported in the four panels below.

Share Volume

	Less than 500 shares	500 – 999 shares	1000 – 1499 shares	1500 - 9999	Total
Floor	3,964,700	8,499,700	4,716,600	93,308,600	110,489,600
PER	58,542,440	64,967,400	22,765,400	215,464,300	361,739,540
All Trades	62,507,140	73,467,100	27,482,000	308,772,900	472,229,140

Percent of Total Volume (%)

	Less than 500 shares	500 – 999 shares	1000 – 1499 shares	1500 - 9999	Average order size
Floor	0.84	1.80	1.00	19.76	23.40
PER	12.40	13.76	4.82	45.63	76.60
All Trades	13.24	15.56	5.82	65.39	100.00

Trade Size (shares)

	Less than 500 shares	500 – 999 shares	1000 – 1499 shares	1500 - 9999	Average order size
Floor	283.76	905.19	1358.08	4038.46	2212.45
PER	250.54	882.46	1346.59	3366.31	931.85
All Trades	252.42	885.03	1348.55	3544.59	1077.82

Time between trades -15 and +15 (in minutes)

	Less than 500 shares	500 – 999 shares	1000 – 1499 shares	1500 - 9999	Average order size
Floor	32.19	27.04	26.28	23.17	26.64
PER	30.44	25.95	28.04	20.68	27.87
All Trades	30.54	26.07	27.74	21.34	27.73

Table 2

Matched Sample Results, All Trades: Quoted half-spread, effective half-spread and realized half-spread, reported in basis points, for matched pairs of floor and PER initiated trades classified by the four trade size categories at the American Stock Exchange during October 2001.

The quoted half-spread is defined as $Quoted\ Half - Spread = (Ask - Bid)/(Bid + Ask)$. The effective half-spread is

$Effective\ Half - Spread = D_{it} \cdot \{[P_0 - (Bid + Ask)/2]/[(Bid + Ask)/2]\}$ where P_0 is the transaction price and D_{it} is an indicator variable that is equal to $+1$ for buyer-initiated trades and is equal to -1 for seller-initiated trades. The realized half-spread for trade t for stock i is the negative of the logarithmic return from the transaction (with the trade price denoted by P_0) to the mid-quote at the time of the fifteenth trade after the transaction denoted by M_{+15}, i.e., $Realized\ Half-Spread = D_{it} \cdot [\ln(P_0 / M_{+15})]$.

The matching is achieved as follows. For each floor trade, we try to locate a matching PER trade. The matching criteria are: (1) trades must be in the same stock, (2) trades must be in the same direction, buy or sell, (3) the execution price of the PER trade must be within 20% of the price of the floor trade, and (4) the size of the PER trade must be within 20% of the size of the floor trade.

Quoted Half-Spread (in basis points)

	Less than 500 shares	500 - 999 shares	1000 – 1499 shares	1500 - 9999 shares	Average
Floor	17.02	16.78	16.77	15.39	16.23
PER	18.18	18.60	19.33	16.23	17.47
All Trades	*-1.16"*	*-1.82"*	*-2.56"*	*-0.84"*	*-1.24"*

Effective Half-Spread (in basis points)

	Less than 500 shares	500 - 999 shares	1000 – 1499 shares	1500 - 9999 shares	Average
Floor	7.26	8.08	9.38	8.47	8.11
PER	9.69	10.97	12.16	10.04	10.27
All Trades	*-2.44"*	*-2.89"*	*-2.78"*	*-1.57"*	*-2.16"*

Realized Half-Spread (in basis points)

	Less than 500 shares	500 - 999 shares	1000 – 1499 shares	1500 - 9999 shares	Average
Floor	-7.20	-3.03	-3.47	-0.33	-3.06
PER	2.51	3.10	3.94	6.33	4.43
All Trades	*-9.71"*	*-6.13"*	*-7.41"*	*-6.67"*	*-7.49"*

[**] Denotes significance at the 1% level

Table 3

Matched Sample Results, Trades with Similar Information Content: Quoted half-spread, effective half-spread and realized half-spread, reported in basis points, for matched pairs of floor and PER initiated trades classified by the four trade size categories at the American Stock Exchange during October 2001.

The quoted half-spread is defined as $Quoted\ Half-Spread = (Ask - Bid)/(Bid + Ask)$. The effective half-spread is

$Effective\ Half-Spread = D_{it} \cdot \{[P_0 - (Bid + Ask)/2]/[(Bid + Ask)/2]\}$ where P_0 is the transaction price and D_{it} is an indicator variable that is equal to $+1$ for buyer-initiated trades and is equal to -1 for seller-initiated trades. The realized half-spread for trade t for stock i is the negative of the logarithmic return from the transaction (with the trade price denoted by P_0) to the mid-quote at the time of the fifteenth trade after the transaction denoted by M_{+15}, i.e., $Realized\ Half-Spread = D_{it} \cdot [\ln(P_0/M_{+15})]$. The matching is achieved as follows. For each floor trade, we try to locate a matching PER trade. The matching criteria are: (1) trades must be in the same stock, (2) trades must be in the same direction, buy or sell, (3) the execution price of the PER trade must be within 20% of the price of the floor trade, and (4) the size of the PER trade must be within 20% of the size of the floor trade. Additionally, the permanent price impact, defined as $Permanent\ Price\ Impact = D_{it} \cdot [\ln(M_{+15}/M_{-15})]$, of the PER trade must be within 20% of that of the floor trade.

Quoted Half-Spread (in basis points)

	Less than 500 shares	500 - 999 shares	1000 – 1499 shares	1500 - 9999 shares	Average
Floor	15.81	15.85	14.96	12.96	14.53
PER	16.66	16.95	16.76	13.54	15.38
All Trades	*-0.85***"	*-1.10***"	*-1.80***"	*-0.58***"	*-0.85***"

Effective Half-Spread (in basis points)

	Less than 500 shares	500 - 999 shares	1000 – 1499 shares	1500 - 9999 shares	Average
Floor	6.83	7.52	7.94	7.02	7.13
PER	8.89	10.16	10.34	8.17	8.94
All Trades	*-2.06***"	*-2.64***"	*-2.40***"	*-1.15***"	*-1.81***"

Realized Half-Spread (in basis points)

	Less than 500 shares	500 - 999 shares	1000 – 1499 shares	1500 - 9999 shares	Average
Floor	-7.14	-4.61	-5.81	-1.72	-4.21
PER	-2.55	0.53	0.87	1.17	-0.09
All Trades	*-4.60***"	*-5.14***"	*-6.68***"	*-2.88***"	*-4.12***"

* Denotes significance at the 5% level

** Denotes significance at the 1% level

Table 4

Matched Sample Results for SPDRS: Quoted half-spread, effective half-spread and realized half-spread, reported in basis points, for matched pairs of floor and PER initiated trades classified by the four trade size categories at the American Stock Exchange during October 2001.

The quoted half-spread is defined as $Quoted\ Half-Spread = (Ask - Bid)/(Bid + Ask)$. The effective half-spread is

$Effective\ Half-Spread = D_{it} \cdot \{[P_0 - (Bid + Ask)/2]/[(Bid + Ask)/2]\}$ where P_0 is the transaction price and D_{it} is an indicator variable that is equal to $+1$ for buyer-initiated trades and is equal to -1 for seller-initiated trades. The realized half-spread for trade t for stock i is the negative of the logarithmic return from the transaction (with the trade price denoted by P_0) to the mid-quote at the time of the fifteenth trade after the transaction denoted by M_{+15}, i.e., $Realized\ Half-Spread = D_{it} \cdot [\ln(P_0/M_{+15})]$.

The matching is achieved as follows. For each floor trade, we try to locate a matching PER trade. The matching criteria are: (1) trades must be in the same direction, buy or sell, (2) the execution price of the PER trade must be within 20% of the price of the floor trade, and (3) the size of the PER trade must be within 20% of the size of the floor trade.

Quoted Half-Spread (in basis points)

	Less than 500 shares	500 - 999 shares	1000 – 1499 shares	1500 - 9999 shares	Average
Floor	4.01	3.91	3.94	3.92	3.93
PER	3.90	4.00	4.04	4.04	4.01
All Trades	*0.11***	*-0.09*	*-0.11*	*-0.12***	*-0.08*

Effective Half-Spread (in basis points)

	Less than 500 shares	500 - 999 shares	1000 – 1499 shares	1500 - 9999 shares	Average
Floor	0.13	0.91	0.70	1.23	0.95
PER	1.84	2.15	2.37	2.34	2.23
All Trades	*-1.70***	*-1.23***	*-1.66***	*-1.11***	*-1.27***

Realized Half-Spread (in basis points)

	Less than 500 shares	500 - 999 shares	1000 – 1499 shares	1500 - 9999 shares	Average
Floor	-0.43	-0.73	0.03	0.14	-0.09
PER	2.11	2.05	2.32	2.02	2.06
All Trades	*-2.54***	*-2.78***	*-2.29***	*-1.88***	*-2.16***

* Denotes significance at the 1% level

Participant Biographies

Brooke Allen is president of MANE Fund Management, Inc., an equity market neutral hedge fund management company. He defines natural market participants as those for whom the market exist, and parasitic participants as those who exist because the markets exist. In his 25 years in the security industry he has been both a natural and parasitic participant, both in New York and Tokyo. He has a BA in Mathematics and an MBA in Finance.

At the time of the conference, **Matthew Andresen** was on the Board of Directors of Lava Trading, a New York trading technology company. Immediately prior to that, Matt served as Head of Global Trading for Sanford C. Bernstein. In that role, he was responsible for all aspects of Bernstein's $300M trading business. He was featured on the cover of Trader's Magazine in October 2003 for his work at Bernstein. Prior to Bernstein, Mr. Andresen served as President and CEO of Island ECN. As one of the first three employees, he built this electronic stock market into the largest in the country. He was responsible for all strategic and operational decisions at Island. In June of 2002, he affected the sale of Island to its largest competitor, Instinet (NASDAQ: INET) in a transaction valued at $568 Million. After the merger, Mr. Andresen assumed the duties of Chief Operating Officer for the combined ECN. He served in that capacity until the end of the year, when he was hired by Sally Krawcheck at Bernstein. Prior to Island, Mr. Andresen was a trader in various capacities for five years.

Mr. Andresen was named as one of the Top 10 executives in Online Finance by Institutional Investor. Crain's Magazine named him one of the Top 40 New Yorkers under the age of 40. Ticker Magazine listed him as one of the Top 100 executives in the Financial world. He has appeared as an expert before many Congressional Committees, on subjects as diverse as Venture Capital in Biotechnology, the future of Electronic Markets, the impact of technology on Commodity markets, and the effect of September 11 on Financial Markets. He is a regular commentator on various financial and news outlets.

Mr. Andresen holds a B.A. in Economics and Political Science from Duke University in Durham, NC. A former world-class fencer, Mr. Andresen was a National Champion, a four-time All-America, a member of dozens of US National Teams, and an alternate for the 1996 US Olympic Team.Theodore Aronson

James J. Angel is Associate Professor of Finance at the McDonough School of Business at Georgetown University. His specialty is the microstructure of securities markets, where he pays special attention to short selling and to microcap issues such as those that trade on the OTCBB and Pink Sheets markets. He has visited over 40 stock or derivative exchanges around the world. For the year 1999-2000 Professor Angel was the Visiting Academic Fellow at the NASD, where he participated in several studies of The Nasdaq Stock Market, Inc. He has served on Nasdaq's OTCBB Advisory Board, and he has served as Chair of the Nasdaq Economic Advisory Board.

After graduating from the California Institute of Technology, he began his career as a Rate Engineer at Pacific Gas and Electric Company. Following an MBA from Harvard Business School, he worked developing equity risk models at BARRA, Inc. "Dr. Jim" earned a Ph.D. in finance from the University of California at Berkeley, and then joined the faculty of Georgetown in 1991. Professor Angel has published in numerous prestigious academic journals, including the *Journal of Finance* and the *Journal of Financial Economics*. He has appeared on many radio and television programs, and is quoted regularly in major newspapers including the *Wall Street Journal*, and the *Financial Times*. Professor Angel has also served as a consultant to broker-dealers, stock markets, and law firms.

Theodore Aronson founded AJO (formerly Aronson+Partners and before that Aronson+Fogler) in 1984. While still a graduate student, Ted joined Drexel Burnham Investment Advisors, where he was a member of its Quantitative Equities Group. This group managed the Revere Fund, the first active SEC-registered fund to employ MPT. Prior to forming AJO, he founded Addison Capital. Ted was past chair of the CFA Institute (formerly AIMR) and is both a CFA charterholder and a Chartered Investment Counselor. He is a trustee of Spelman College and on its investment committee. He was a Lecturer in Finance at The Wharton School. Ted is involved with portfolio management, administration, and marketing.

Eric Barret graduated from Duke in 1997. He has worked at Euro Brokers, Maxcor as a fixed income and derivatives trader, as a broker at First Union Securities Inc. and a sales manager at GL TRADE, an electronic trading software vendor. Mr. Barret is currently Director of Global Electronic Trading Services at CIBC World Markets Corp. in New York, a full service broker dealer. The GETS group focuses on direct market access, algorithmic trading, program trading, connectivity and cross border execution services for institutions and other broker dealers.

George H. Bodine is currently Director of Trading for General Motors Investment Management Corporation (GMIMCo). He is responsible for worldwide equity and derivative trading relating to GMIMCo's internal investment funds. Prior to assuming his current position in September, 1996, Mr. Bodine was Vice President of Schwab Institutional overseeing equities and options trading for the small to mid-tier investment advisors. Preceding that, he spent his career with Equitable/Alliance Capital starting in 1972.

Mr. Bodine received his BS in Psychology in 1972 from Syracuse University and MS in Business Management in 1979 from Central Michigan University. Mr. Bodine is currently a member of the Securities Trader Association and National Organization of Investment Professionals. He is a former member of both the NYSE and AMEX Institutional Traders Advisory Committees. He is on the Advisory Board of the Ballentine Investment Institute at the M. J. Whitman School of Management at Syracuse University.

Michael Buek is a principal at The Vanguard Group. He is trader and index portfolio manager in the Quantitative Equity Group which manages over $275 billion. He joined Vanguard in 1987 and has been on the trading desk since 1991. Mr. Buek, CFA, graduated from the University of Vermont in 1987 and received an MBA from Villanova University in 1993.

Matthew Celebuski is a Managing Director at JPMorgan. Matt's responsibilities include electronic execution services and strategy. Matt has worked in all aspects of equity trading at JPMorgan and much the same at Merrill Lynch prior to JPMorgan. Matt has worked in Hedge Funds, run global derivative groups and started his career in futures and options research. Matt is a board member of CISDM (Center for International Securities and Derivative Markets), an editor of the Journal of Alternative Investments and a board member of curriculum and exam committees of the Chartered Alternative Investment Analyst Designation.

Christopher R. Concannon is Executive Vice President, Transaction Services for The NASDAQ Stock Market, Inc., a role he assumed in October 2003. Mr. Concannon joined NASDAQ in May 2003 as Executive Vice President of Strategy and Business Development.

Prior to joining NASDAQ, Mr. Concannon was President of Instinet Clearing Services, Inc., where he managed the clearing and execution services business offered by Instinet Clearing to numerous broker dealer clients. Throughout his career with Instinet, Mr. Concannon also served as Special Counsel and Senior Vice President of Business Development, most recently coordinating and advising senior management on the integration of Instinet and Island ECN.

Prior to the merger of Instinet and Island, Mr. Concannon was Special Counsel and Vice President of Business Development for Island, where he was responsible for formulating, planning and executing the firm's global and domestic strategies. While at Island, Mr. Concannon worked closely with the firm's strategic partners and investors, identified relationships with potential strategic partners and investors and managed the day-to-day activities of Island's Business Development Department. Mr. Concannon joined The Island, ECN in 1999 as Vice President and Associate General Counsel.

Prior to joining Island, he was an associate at Morgan, Lewis & Bockius LLP in their New York and Washington offices. From 1994-1997 he was an attorney with the U.S. Securities and Exchange Commission in the Division of Market Regulation where he specialized in the review and approval of the rules of the various self-regulatory organizations, the regulation of securities underwriting and the regulation of the clearance and settlement of securities transactions.

Mr. Concannon began his career with the American Stock Exchange, where he served as a Legislative Analyst from 1992-1995, lobbying Congress and the Administration on a variety of securities related issues. Mr. Concannon received a B.A. from the Catholic University of America in 1989, an M.B.A. from St. John's University in 1991, and a J.D. from the Columbus School of Law, the Catholic University of America in 1994. He is a member of the New York Bar, New Jersey Bar and the District of Columbia Bar.

Paul Davis is a managing director at TIAA-CREF Investment Management LLC. TIAA-CREF, is a national financial services leader and the premier retirement system for higher education and research employees.

Further information can be found at http://www.tiaa-cref.org. Davis joined TIAA-CREF in 1983 after working at Prùdential Securities in New York. Before his career on Wall Street, he taught mathematics at Lehigh University, Manhattanville College and West Virginia University. He has an undergraduate degree from West Virginia University and a doctorate in mathematices from Carnegie Mellon University.

Thomas K. Doyle, Sr., is a 34-year veteran of the institutional equity and option business. His career started at Pershing & Co. (now a subsidiary of The Bank of New York) where he helped launch Pershing's operations on the Chicago Board Options Exchange (CBOE) in 1973. He was a member of the CBOE during 1975-76 and became the youngest partner ever at Pershing. Tom served on various option exchange committees on both of the CBOE and the American Stock Exchange. Tom resigned from Pershing in 1980.

During 1980, Tom became a shareholder of Rochdate Securities Corporation. There he served in the roles of COO and co-CEO. From a base of $250,000 in revenues, Tom was instrumental in all aspects as the firm grew to $25 million in revenues when he departed in 1997. In particular, Tom was the head trader and facilitator for soft-dollar relationships and commission recapture programs on behalf of the country's largest institutional investors. He created systems for tracking execution performances and was a speaker/panelist at various industry forums. Tom's system furthered the examination of best execution to the specific level of the desk trader and the floor broker on each transaction.

Alfred Eskandar heads Liquidnet's marketing and public relations activities. Prior to joining Liquidnet in 2000, he helped launch Securities Industry News (S.I.N.), the leading publication for securities services professionals. Thomson Financial Services (TFS) acquired the publication in 1996. Alfred spent the next four years developing an international executive conference business, as well as heading up business development for the operations, trading and technology division of TFS's Investment Marketing Group. Alfred has 10 years of financial media experience and holds a BBA in Finance and Economics from Baruch College.

Robert Fagenson has spent his entire career at the New York Stock Exchange. He currently serves as Vice Chairman of Van der Moolen Specialists USA, the fourth largest specialist firm on the NYSE, trading more than 400 listed securities. In June 2000 he merged his own specialist firm, Fagenson Frankel & Streicher, with Van der Moolen. The firm's parent is the global trading firm, Van der Moolen N.V., which is based in the

Netherlands and whose ADR's were listed on the New York Stock Exchange on October 18, 2001 (NYSE - VDM).

He has been a Member of the New York Stock Exchange since 1973. He served as Floor Official from 1985 to 1987 and a Floor Governor from 1987 to 1993. In 1993 he was elected to the Board of Directors of the NYSE and served in that capacity for six years, most recently as Vice Chairman in 1998 and 1999. He was re-elected to the NYSE Board, after a four year absence, in June 2003, and resigned from that position in December 2003, when the NYSE Board was reconstituted with only public Directors. He has served as a member and chairman of several NYSE committees and is currently a member of the Technology Planning and Oversight Committee. He has served as Chairman of the Specialist Association at the New York Stock Exchange and has served as its Washington liaison in the nation's capital for the past ten years.

Mr. Fagenson serves as a director of two public companies, Rentway, Inc. (NYSE – RWY) and Cash Technologies Corp (AMEX – TQ). In addition, he is a Vice President and Director of New York Services for the Handicapped, Treasurer and Director of the NYPD Centurion Foundation, Director of the Federal Law Enforcement Officers Association Foundation and a member of the Board of the NYC Police Museum. He also serves in a voluntary capacity on board and committees of many civic, social and community organizations. Mr. Fagenson received his B.S. degree in finance and transportation sciences from Syracuse University in 1970. He is a lifetime resident of Manhattan where he lives with his wife of 30 years, Margaret. They have two grown daughters and one 8 ½ pound toy poodle.

Reto Francioni is President and Chairman of the Board of SWX-Group (Swiss Stock Exchange, Eurex, virt-x, STOXX and EXFEED). Prior to assuming his current position in May, 2002, he was Co-CEO of Consors Discount Broker AG, Nuremberg. In 1993, he was named to the Executive board of Deutsche Börse AG, where he was responsible for its entire cash market. In 1999, he became Deputy Chief Executive Officer. He was an initiator of the exchange's thrust towards internationalization.

Earlier in his career, he held management positions in the securities exchange and banking industry, and was a director of the finance division at Hoffmann LaRoche AG, Basel. Reto Francioni has a law degree and Ph.D. in law from Zurich University and is Professor of Economics and Finance at Zicklin School of Business, Baruch College, The City University of New York. He is the co-author of the book 'Equity Markets in Action'.

Dr. **William C. Freund** served as the New York Stock Exchange's Senior Vice President and Chief Economist for 18 years (1968-1986). He was the New York Stock Exchange Professor of Economics at Pace University's Lubin School of Business from 1986 to 2001. He was Chairman of Pace University's Graduate Department of Economics and International Business from 1986-1993. Since 1993, he has been Director of Pace University's William C. Freund Center for the Study of Securities Markets.

From 1952 to 1962, he was Economist for the Prudential Insurance Company of America. From 1962 to 1965, he was Associate Professor of Finance at NYU's Graduate School of Business. He returned to Prudential as Chief Economist and Director of Investment Research between 1965 and 1968.

Dr. Freund's Ph.D. degree is from Columbia University. For twenty years, he was an economic adviser (pro bono) to four governors of New Jersey. He has served on a number of corporate boards of directors, including Ecogen and US Life Corp. He is author of several books including <u>Investment Fundamentals</u>, and co-author of <u>People and Productivity</u>. He has written chapters for numerous other books and has authored a large number of articles.

Adena Friedman is Executive Vice President of Corporate Strategy and Data Products for the NASDAQ Stock Market, Inc. Friedman's responsibilities include identifying and developing strategic opportunities for the world's largest electronic stock market. They also include maintaining the integrity of all market data disseminated to the public and working with NASDAQ Technology Services to create new data products to serve the industry's information needs. Additionally, Friedman serves as the senior administrator for NASDAQ in its capacity as the Exclusive Securities Information Processor for NASDAQ-listed securities.

Friedman joined NASDAQ in 1993. She served for one year as a Senior Vice President of NASDAQ Data Products. In addition, she served for three years as a Director, and subsequently, Vice President, of NASDAQ Trading and Market Services, the division of NASDAQ that supported Market Makers and other market participants. She was responsible for the strategy and successful operation of the OTC Bulletin Board®, a quotation facility for unlisted stocks; the Mutual Fund Quotation Service, a net asset value reporting tool for money-management firms; and NASDAQTrader.com, the central NASDAQ Web site for member firms and buy-side traders.

Prior to that position, Friedman served as Marketing Manager in NASDAQ Trading and Market Services. Additionally, she developed the department's annual budget and financial plan and participated in ongoing strategic planning initiatives. Friedman earned an M.B.A., with honors, from Owen Graduate School of Management, Vanderbilt University, in Nashville, TN. She holds a B.A. in Political Science from Williams College in Massachusetts.

Robert C. Gasser has served as Chief Executive Officer, NYFIX Millennium, our 80%-owned broker dealer subsidiary, since October 2001. Mr. Gasser is also President of NYFIX Transaction Services and NYFIX Clearing Corporation. Prior to joining NYFIX, Mr. Gasser was Head of U.S. Equity Trading for JP Morgan, an investment bank. During his tenure at JP Morgan, Mr. Gasser served on various industry committees, including the NASDAQ Quality of Markets Committee and the NYSE Upstairs Traders Advisory Committee. In addition, he directed the firm's investment in NYFIX Millennium and Archipelago, where he actively served on the Board of Managers. Mr. Gasser holds a Bachelor of Science degree in Foreign Service from Georgetown University, School of Foreign Service.

Allan D. Grody has been involved in the financial industry for nearly 40 years. He was an early innovator in technology within the banking, securities and investment industries, continued to serve the financial industry as the founding partner of Coopers & Lybrand's financial services consulting practice, and later went on to found businesses in financial planning and internet based financial services. He has authored articles and studies on electronic trading, financial markets and risk management. He founded and taught a unique risk management systems course at NYU's Stern School of Business. Throughout his career he has represented stock, options and futures exchanges as an expert witness. He is now a private consultant and operates a financial services development company, Financial InterGroup. He holds a B.S. degree in mathematics from the City University of New York.

Christopher J. Heckman is a Managing Director at Investment Technology Group Inc. He is a member of ITG's Executive Committee and is co-head of US Sales and Trading. Christopher joined ITG in January 1991 as a sales trader and became manager of institutional sales and trading in January 1997. Prior to ITG, Christopher worked on the US Equity desk at Salomon Brothers from 1987 - 1991. During that period, Christopher was involved in program trading, both in the United States and Japan. Christopher has a BS in computer science from St. Johns University.

Arthur R. Hogan III is Chief Market Analyst at Jefferies & Company, an institutional brokerage firm focusing on equity, high yield convertible and international securities. He is also Manager of the Boston office at Jefferies where he heads the equity trading effort.

Mr. Hogan appears regularly on CNBC, CNN, CNN-FN, Bloomberg-TV, and Reuters TV, as well as being often quoted in The Wall Street Journal, The New York Times and Financial Times. Prior to joining Jefferies, Mr. Hogan was a part of the institutional equity trading departments at Morgan Stanley and Dean Witter. From 1984 to 1993, Mr. Hogan was Vice President of Fidelity's Capital Markets Division during which time he spearheaded Fidelity's floor brokerage operation at the Boston Stock Exchange. Mr. Hogan received a Bachelor's Degree from the University of Vermont in 1983, where he majored in Economics and Political Science. Mr. Hogan is married with two children and currently resides in Duxbury, Massachusetts.

Catherine R. Kinney, 53, has been president and co-chief operating officer of the New York Stock Exchange since January 2002. Prior to her current position, Mrs. Kinney was group executive vice president since June 1995, overseeing the Exchange's competitive position and relationships with its listed companies, member firms and institutions as well as the Exchange Traded Funds, and Fixed Income divisions. Prior to that, since 1986, she was responsible for managing trading-floor operations and technology. Joining the NYSE in 1974, Mrs. Kinney has worked in several departments, including regulation, sales and marketing, and technology planning. Mrs. Kinney is a member of the board of the New York Stock Exchange Foundation, the Depository Trust & Clearing Corporation (DTCC), the Board of Directors at Georgetown University and the Board of Junior Achievement of New York. She served on the Board of the Metropolitan Life Insurance Co. from 2002-2004. Mrs. Kinney graduated Magna Cum Laude from Iona College and completed the Advanced Management Program, Harvard Graduate School of Business. She has received honorary degrees from Georgetown University and Rosemont College.

Richard Korhammer, CEO and co-founder of Lava Trading Inc., is a proven successful Wall Street veteran with extensive experience working with some of the largest investment banks and financial services firms. Prior to co-founding Lava, Richard ran his own management consulting firm where he provided strategic, technical and advisory services predominantly focusing on trading departments of many leading investment banks including Deutsche Bank, JP Morgan Chase, Morgan Stanley and Salomon Brothers, among others. Richard began his career with NeXT Computers, founded by Steve Jobs, CEO of Apple Computers. At NeXT, he worked closely with Wall Street firms in the analysis of NeXTStep's custom application development architecture in the area of proprietary trading solutions.

Richard is a graduate of Princeton University and holds a B.S.E. in Computer Science and Electrical Engineering. He is a member of the NASDAQ UTP Advisory Committee and is a recipient of several honors, including the New York Ten Award and the Ernst & Young Entrepreneur of the Year Award.

Michael LaBranche is the Chairman, CEO and President of LaBranche & Co Inc. since its inception as a public corporation in August 1999. LaBranche & Co Inc. is the parent of LaBranche & Co., a New York Stock Exchange Specialist firm since 1924. A graduate of the University of Vermont, Mr. LaBranche joined the firm in 1977 and became a New York Stock Exchange member as a Specialist in 1978. Mr. LaBranche has served on the Management Committee and Executive Operating Committee of LaBranche & Co. since 1988 and as the Chairman of the Executive Operating Committee since 1996. He is currently Chairman of LaBranche & Co Inc.'s Executive Management Committee. He serves as a Governor of the New York Stock Exchange and is a member of the New York Stock Exchange's Market Performance Committee. He is a board member of Lava Trading and the Securities Industry Automation Corporation (SIAC).

Robert McCooey spearheaded the founding of The Griswold Company in 1988. He also orchestrated its transformation from a traditional 'two-dollar' broker into a large, sophisticated, technologically advanced, Direct Access agency execution firm. Griswold serves both prominent buy-side institutions and many developing organizations, with unrivaled efficiency.

Bob currently serves on the New York Stock Exchange Board of Executives, which he was appointed to in December 2003. Bob served eight terms as a New York Stock Exchange Floor Official, and two terms as a Senior Floor Official. Bob currently serves on the Exchange's Market Structure Working Group and its Market Performance, Market Information, Diversity and Continuing Education committees. He has also served on the

Allocations, Hearing Board, Governor Selection, Decimalization and Dual Quotations committees. He is past President of the Alliance of Floor Brokers and past President and Trustee of its Floor Member Emergency Fund. Additionally, he previously served as a member of the Trading Issues Committee of the Securities Traders Association. In 2000, he was elected to the prestigious National Organization of Investment Professionals. He has testified about market structure and Reg NMS before Congress three times in the last two years, including twice before the House Committee on Financial Services and once before the Senate Committee on Banking, Housing and Urban Affairs. A regular guest on CNBC and CNNfn, Bob is often quoted in The Wall Street Journal and other news outlets covering stock market activity. Bob is a member of the Board of Directors of Iona Preparatory School, his alma mater, and of the St. Vincent's Hospital, Westchester. He is active in numerous other charitable organizations in New York. A graduate of The College of Holy Cross, Bob holds Series 7, 12, 24 and 63 licenses. He lives in Westchester County, New York, with his wife and six children.

Mary McDermott-Holland is Senior Vice President of Trading at Franklin Portfolio Associates (a Mellon Financial Company) in Boston, Massachusetts. She has held a variety of positions since joining the firm in June 1982 and currently oversees trading for the firm. Mary currently serves as Chairman of the Security Traders Association (STA). She has also served STA as Co-Chair of the Trading Issues Committee, as Co-Chair of the Institutional Committee, Chairman of the Conference Committee, Chairman of the Technology Committee and Chairman of the Economic Education Committee. Mary is a former member of NASDAQ's Institutional Traders Advisory Council having been a founding member of that committee and she served, as it's inaugural Chairman from 1998-2001 and as a committee member thorough 2003. Mary also serves on the Board of the Boston Stock Exchange and on the New York Stock Exchange Institutional Traders Advisory Committee and has served on NYSE's Allocation Committee. Mary is a former Chairman of the Electronic Products Advisory Committee to the Boston Stock Exchange, and a former Co-Chair of NASDAQ's Quality of Markets Committee. Mary is also a member of Trader Forum's Advisory Committee, a member of the National Organization of Investment Professionals, and a member of the Investment Company Institute Equity Markets Advisory Committee. Mary served as a member of the Boston Security Traders Association board 16 years, 11 as Treasurer and as President of that organization in 1993.

Doreen Mogavero has been a member of the NYSE since 1980. Her securities industry experience includes corporate buybacks, institutional block trading, risk arbitrage and convertible arbitrage. Her series registrations include the 7, 63 and 12. Doreen was recently appointed to the Board of Executives of the NYSE and also serves as one of only two floor representatives appointed to a subcommittee of the Independent Board called the Regulation Enforcement and Listing Standards Committee. She previously served as the Vice President of the Organization of Independent Floor Brokers (OIFB) and Treasurer and Trustee of the Floor Members Emergency Fund (FMEF). Doreen was a member of the NYSE Hearing Panel for 22 years and has served 12 terms as an NYSE Floor Official.

Doreen has appeared as a guest market commentator on CNBC and CNN-FN. She frequently speaks and participates in panel discussions at industry conferences. She is the New York Area Coordinator for the National Italian American Foundation (NIAF). She is involved with the Financial Women's Association of New York (FWA), is a member of the Security Traders Association of New York (STANY) and is currently a member of the Security Traders Association (STA) Trading Issues Committee.

William O'Brien is Senior Vice President of NASDAQ Market Data Distribution within the NASDAQ Data Products Division. As one of NASDAQ's four primary businesses, Data Products maintains the integrity of all market data disseminated to the public and works with NASDAQ Technology Services to create new data products to serve the industry's information needs. In this position, Mr. O'Brien is responsible for the creation and dissemination of valuable information from the quoting and trading of NASDAQ® securities.

Mr. O'Brien was formerly Chief Operating Officer of Brut, LLC. He helped lead Brut through its September 2004 acquisition by NASDAQ. Prior to serving as COO of BRUT, Mr. O'Brien served at Brut as Senior Vice President and General Counsel, with responsibilities that included management of Brut's legal affairs, regulatory strategy and Compliance Department.

Edward J. Nicoll is Chief Executive Officer of Instinet Group Incorporated, through affiliates, the largest global electronic agency securities broker serving institutional investors in U.S. trading venues including NASDAQ and the NYSE, and almost 30 securities markets around the globe. He was appointed to the position in September 2002 following the merger of Instinet Group and Island Holding Company. Prior to joining Instinet Group, Mr. Nicoll was Chairman and CEO of Datek Online, a leading online broker serving individual investors, and Chairman of Island Holding Company, a technology leader in electronic marketplaces. Mr. Nicoll was previously a co-founder and President of Waterhouse Investor Services, one of the nation's largest discount brokerage firms.

Mr. Nicoll is a Trustee of the Institute for Advanced Study in Princeton, NJ, dedicated entirely to fundamental research and scholarship across a wide range of fields. He is also a Trustee of the Manhattan Institute, a think tank whose mission is to develop and disseminate new ideas that foster greater economic choice and individual responsibility. In addition, Mr. Nicoll is currently a director of Gerson Lehrman Group and a graduate of Yale Law School.

Michael Pagano has conducted several empirical analyses related to various issues in market microstructure, risk management, cost of capital estimation, interest rate determination, as well as capital allocation in the financial services industry. He has published in numerous finance journals such as the Journal of Financial Economics, Journal of Banking and Finance, Journal of Portfolio Management, and the Financial Analysts Journal. Dr. Pagano also has been a Fulbright Scholar at the University of Costa Rica and has received awards for teaching and academic scholarship.

Prior to earning his doctorate and joining the Villanova University faculty, Dr. Pagano spent over 10 years in the financial services industry. He holds the Chartered Financial Analyst (CFA®) designation and has experience both in commercial lending activities at Citibank and in investment valuation analysis at a financial consulting firm, International Capital Markets Corp., as well as Reuters PLC. In addition to his duties at Villanova University, Dr. Pagano has been a consultant to several companies including Citibank, PaineWebber, Fidelity Investments, GTE Investments, Philadelphia Suburban Corp., and Bank Julius Baer.

Brett Redfearn is a Senior Managing Director at Bear Stearns in the Institutional Equities division focusing on market structure strategy. In that role, Brett examines how new technologies, regulations and business trends are changing the equity trading business. His responsibilities include: (1) helping Bear Stearns develop external public policy positions on market structure issues, (2) addressing market structure related implications and business responses related to a Bear Stearns' equity trading operations; and, (3) authoring Commentaries and analyses on changes and developments in market structure for internal and external consumption. Much of his current focus relates to Regulation NMS and the NYSE's Hybrid market proposal. Prior to Bear Stearns, Brett was at the American Stock Exchange, where he was Senior

Vice President of Business Strategy & Equity Order Flow. Brett's department ran the Amex's equity transactions business and, as such, oversaw the Amex's efforts in relationship management (with buy and sell-side trading desks), competitive research, and strategic initiatives. Brett's latest focus at the Amex was in trying to help the Amex revamp its technology platform and business offering to better compete in an electronic trading environment. Brett is a regular speaker at industry events and a member of the Security Traders Association. He received his M.A. from the New School for Social Research in New York and his B.A. from The Evergreen State College in Olympia Washington.

Richard A. Rosenblatt is Founder, President and Chief Executive Officer of Rosenblatt Securities. He has thirty-four years of securities industry experience, twenty-nine as a New York Stock Exchange member. He is currently an NYSE Executive Floor Official, and spent six years as an NYSE Governor, and four years as an NYSE Floor Official. He originated the first automated order delivery system allowing non-member firms direct access to the NYSE through DOT, and aided the development and implementation of the NYSE's Broker Booth Support System (BBSS).

He is presently serving on the NYSE Allocation Committee and Hearing Board. His other financial and community involvements are: Founder and first President of the Organization of Independent Floor Brokers; Founder and first Chairman of Trustees of the NYSE Floor Members Emergency Fund; Founder and Director of NYSE Fallen Heroes Fund (which provides financial assistance and support to the families of New York City fire and police personnel killed in the line of duty); Founder and Director of Floor Members Outreach Program (a New York Stock Exchange floor-based, adhoc service group providing emergency assistance for members of the financial community seeking help for addictive and substance abuse related problems); and Vice Chair of Board of Trustees, Mercy College.

Jim Ross has spent 15 years in the electronic financial services industry. He is currently CEO of MatchPoint Trading Inc.

As a senior executive at Instinet, Jim was the driving force behind building, developing, promoting and ultimately, leading Instinet's global crossing business. In addition to the daily crossing operations and sales, Jim was involved in strategy and new business development initiatives. Jim was central to the establishment of the first of it's kind Japanese Crossing joint venture between Instinet and Nikko Salomon Smith Barney; a Bermuda Stock Exchange Crossing business; a global benchmark crossing business; a

FX Cross joint venture with Citibank and a pre-market VWAP cross called Market Match. In his final years at Instinet, Jim also oversaw Instinet's Institutional and Strategic Global Sales effort focusing on maximizing and leveraging the various product offerings to its strategic business clients.

In January of 2003, Jim and a team of former Instinet colleagues joined Burlington Capital Markets in order to create and develop a call market business dedicated to addressing issues pertaining to low-hit rates and uncertain execution quality in the crossing industry. In June of 2003, Burlington launched BLOX: its first and the first same day trade date cross in the after-hours environment(at 4:45pm). He is a frequent speaker on industry panels and at conferences regarding market structure and call market trading.

Craig A. Rothfeld is Chief Operating Officer with W.J. Bonfanti, Inc. His responsibilities include overseeing the day to day finance, accounting, compliance, and business development operations of the Company. Mr. Rothfeld is a Shareholder of WJB and joined the firm on a full-time basis several years ago after successfully completing and advising the company on a $2.4 million private placement transaction.

Mr. Rothfeld has extensive capital markets experience as a former Coordinator of Capital Markets for Conectiv where he focused on Debt Refinancings, Stranded Cost Securitization, Commercial Paper programs and State Regulatory and Compliance Issues and as a Vice President of Investments with First Albany Corporation's Private Wealth Management Group. Mr. Rothfeld began his career in public accounting at Arthur Andersen working on Form S-3 Registration Statements and auditing international consolidations for public companies.

Mr. Rothfeld is a Certified Public Accountant, possesses an M.B.A. with concentrations in Finance and International Business from the Leonard N. Stern School of Business at NYU, and a B.S. in Accounting from the University at Albany. He was instrumental in preparation and compilation of the 1999 Survey of Information Technology Firms Operating Results, was Morgan Stanley's guest Panel Speaker at the 2001 IMN ABS West Conference for Re-ignited Power, Utility Stranded Cost Securitization, and is an Advisory Board Member & Lecturer at Oklahoma State University and the NYSE on various Wall Street topics. Additionally, he is an Allied Member of the NYSE and possesses his Series 7, 14, 27, and 63 securities licenses.

Mr. Rothfeld lives on the East Side of Manhattan with his wife Carrie who is an Architect and their daughter Stella where he and they enjoy long distance running, arts and architecture, reading novels and traveling to foreign countries.

Lanny A. Schwartz is Executive Vice President and General Counsel at Philadelphia Stock Exchange, Inc. Previously, Mr. Schwartz was a Managing Director & Counsel at Bankers Trust Company in New York and an attorney in the New York and London offices of Cleary, Gottlieb, Steen & Hamilton. He also served as a Lecturer in Law at Columbia University Law School for 3 years. Mr. Schwartz is an experienced speaker on securities market issues, including at the NASD-Aresty Institute program held at the Wharton School. Mr. Schwartz holds a Bachelor of Arts degree in Oriental Studies from the University of Pennsylvania and a Juris Doctor from New York University School of Law.

Robert A. Schwartz is Marvin M. Speiser Professor of Finance and University Distinguished Professor in the Zicklin School of Business, Baruch College, CUNY. Before joining the Baruch faculty in 1997, he was Professor of Finance and Economics and Yamaichi Faculty Fellow at New York University's Leonard N. Stern School of Business, where he had been a member of the faculty since 1965. Professor Schwartz received his Ph.D. in Economics from Columbia University. His research is in the area of financial economics, with a primary focus on the structure of securities markets. He has published numerous journal articles and eleven books, including Equity Markets in Action: The Fundamentals of Liquidity, Market Structure and Trading, Wiley & Sons, 2004, and Reshaping the Equity Markets: A Guide for the 1990s, Harper Business, 1991 (reissued by Business One Irwin, 1993). He has served as a consultant to various market centers including the New York Stock Exchange, the American Stock Exchange, NASDAQ, the London Stock Exchange, Instinet, the Arizona Stock Exchange, Deutsche Börse, and the Bolsa Mexicana. From April 1983 to April 1988, he was an associate editor of The Journal of Finance, and he is currently an associate editor of the Review of Quantitative Finance and Accounting, the Review of Pacific Basin Financial Markets and Policies, and The Journal of Entrepreneurial Finance & Business Ventures, and is a member of the advisory board of International Finance. In December 1995, Professor Schwartz was named the first chairman of NASDAQ's Economic Advisory Board, and he served on the EAB until Spring 1999.

Jamie Selway is Chairman and Managing Director of White Cap Trading LLC, a brokerage firm located in New York. Jamie and his partners founded White Cap to provide institutional investors with cost-effective, unconflicted brokerage. White Cap accomplishes this through an agency-only approach and an expertise in electronic markets. In addition, White Cap offers insight on the changing structure of marketplaces, so that its clients are well-positioned to maximize execution quality and minimize information leakage.

Before forming White Cap, Jamie was Chief Economist at Archipelago Holdings, L.L.C., the Chicago-based electronic brokerage firm and creator of the first totally open, fully electronic U.S. stock exchange. Jamie served a variety of functions at Archipelago, including strategy, quantitative research, regulatory and governmental liaison, and new business development.

Jamie's other professional experiences include the Equity Derivatives Research group of Goldman, Sachs & Co. (New York), three years in the Economic Research group at the National Association of Securities Dealers, Inc. (Washington), and two years at Economists, Inc. (Washington). Jamie has written articles published in both industry press and academic journals, and has been quoted in the Wall Street Journal and the Financial Times. He currently serves on the Users Subcommittee of the Intermarket Trading System and the Advisory Committee of the NASDAQ UTP Plan. Jamie holds an M.S. in Financial Mathematics from the University of Chicago and a B.A. in Mathematics and European History from Washington & Lee University, Phi Beta Kappa.

Robert B. Shapiro is the Director of Trading at Iridian Asset Management LLC in Westport, Conn. The mid & large cap value manager, which was recently acquired by the Bank of Ireland, oversees more than $10 billion in assets for its institutional client base. Rob manages the firm's four person trading desk. Prior to joining Iridian, Rob was a Managing Director and Board Member at Enskilda Securities in New York, and a Managing Director of Kempen & Co. USA. He began his career at Arnhold and S. Bleichroeder in New York, where he served as a senior foreign equity position trader, senior global research salesman and founder of WorldVest Inc, an independent on-line international research subsidiary. Rob is on The Advisory Board of Trader Forum & received a BBA in Business Administration from the University of Michigan, Ann Arbor.

Michael Simon is SVP, Legal and Regulatory, General Counsel, Secretary and Chief Regulatory Officer of ISE. From 1993 to 1998, Mr. Simon was 'Of Counsel' to Milbank, Tweed, Hadley & McCloy. He had previously been Senior Attorney and an Associate with the firm since 1988. Mr. Simon practiced in the firm's Corporate and Banking Department where for six years he had primary responsibility for representation of the New York Stock Exchange, focusing on corporate listings, market structure and regulation. From 1986 to 1988, Mr. Simon was Vice President and Associate General Counsel of the National Securities Clearing Corporation, where he handled general corporate and regulatory matters. There, he also worked on international clearance and settlement and on the development of the first clearance and settlement facility for government securities. From 1978 to 1986, Mr. Simon was with the U.S. Securities and Exchange Commission where he was Assistant Director for Over-the-Counter Market Regulation and Structure. Mr. Simon is a graduate of the University of Pittsburgh School of Law and the University of Rochester, and is a member of the American Bar Association.

Dr. **Benn Steil** is Director of International Economics at the Council on Foreign Relations in New York. He is also the Editor of International Finance (Blackwell Publishers); a co-founder and director of Efficient Frontiers LLC, a markets consultancy; a nonexecutive director of the virt-x stock exchange in London; and a member of the European Shadow Financial Regulatory Committee. Until November 1998, he was Director of the International Economics Programme at the Royal Institute of International Affairs in London. Prior to his appointment at the Institute in 1992, he held a Lloyd's of London Tercentenary Research Fellowship at Nuffield College, Oxford, where he received his PhD in Economics.

Dr. Steil has written and spoken widely on securities trading and market regulation. His research and market commentary are regularly covered in publications such as the Wall Street Journal, Financial Times, New York Times, International Herald Tribune, USA Today, The Economist, Barrons, Business Week, Forbes, Fortune, Time, Newsweek, Securities Industry News, Financial News, Traders Magazine, and Reuters and Bloomberg online. Among his books are a critically acclaimed study of The European Equity Markets and a major text on Institutional Investors, as well as edited volumes on cross-border antitrust (Antitrust Goes Global) and the economics of innovation (Technological Innovation and Economic Performance). Most recently he published a major policy study entitled Building a Transatlantic Securities Market, which has been widely reviewed in the North American and European financial press, and has been the topic of numerous conferences in North America and Europe. His next book is called Financial Statecraft: The Role of Financial Markets in American Foreign Policy, which will be published by Yale University Press later this year.

Wayne Wagner is a co-founder of Plexus Group, a Los Angeles based firm that provides implementation evaluation and advisory services to U.S. and Global money managers, brokerage firms and pension plan sponsors. Mr. Wagner and Plexus Group were chosen as the 1999 Consultant of the Year by Plan Sponsor Magazine. Investment News named him one of the 'Power Elite 25' for 2001. Plexus Group is an independent subsidiary of JPMorgan Investor Services Company, a division of JPMorgan Chase.

Mr. Wagner is author and editor of The Complete Guide to Securities Transactions: Improving Performance and Reducing Costs, John Wiley & Sons, 1989. His most recent publishing effort is a popular investment book written with friend Al Winnikoff entitled MILLIONAIRE: the simplest explanation of how an index fund can turn your lunch money into a fortune; Renaissance Books, 2001. He has written and spoken frequently on many trading and investment subjects. He has received two Graham and Dodd Awards from the Financial Analysts Journal for excellence in financial writing.

Mr. Wagner served as a Regent of the Financial Analysts Seminar and served on the AIMR Blue Ribbon Task Force on Soft Dollars and the AIMR Best Execution Task Force.

Mr. Wagner was a founding partner of Wilshire Associates and served as Chief Investment Officer of Wilshire Asset Management. Earlier, Mr. Wagner participated in the design and operation of the first index funds at Wells Fargo Bank. In an earlier century Mr. Wagner earned a MS in Statistics from Stanford University and a BBA in Management Science/Finance from the University of Wisconsin.

Avner Wolf is the Executive Director of University International Programs. Professor Wolf received his PH.D. from Columbia University in Finance. His research is in the areas of derivative Financial Markets and Market Microstructure. He has published numerous papers in academic as well as professional journals and worked with Financial Institutions world wide on a variety of projects on derivatives.

INDEX